CHRISTABI

by the same author

fiction
TICKET TO RIDE
BLACKEYES

plays
SUFFICIENT CARBOHYDRATE

TV screenplays
THE SINGING DETECTIVE

CHRISTABEL

DENNIS POTTER

Adapted from
The Past is Myself
by Christabel Bielenberg

faber and faber
LONDON · BOSTON

First published in 1988
by Faber and Faber Limited
3 Queen Square London WC1N 3AU

Photoset by Parker Typesetting Service Leicester
Printed in Great Britain by
Richard Clay Ltd Bungay Suffolk

This screenplay is based on *The Past is Myself*
by Christabel Bielenberg, published by Corgi.

British Library Cataloguing in Publication Data

Potter, Dennis *1935*–
Christabel
I. Title
822'.914
ISBN 0-571-15437-9

Christabel was first shown on BBC Television in November 1988. The cast was as follows:

CHRISTABEL	Elizabeth Hurley
PETER	Stephen Dillon
MR BURTON	Geoffrey Palmer
MRS BURTON	Ann Bell
US AIRMAN	Dennis Christopher
ADAM	Nigel Le Vaillant
LEXI	Suzan Crowley
LANGE	Ralph Brown
BAUSCH	Jim Carter
FRAU MUCKLE	Pat Heywood
LANGBEHN	Sam Kelly
SS MAN	Andrew Wilde
ILSE	Jessica Turner
VOLK	Richard Ireson
KREUZE	David Lyon
BOTHO	Hugh Simon
NEISSE	John Burgess
AUNT ULLA	Renny Lister
ALBRECHT	Adrian Rawlins
OLD LADY	Edna Doré
PROFESSOR BAUER	Guy Deghy
FRAU LANGE	Joanne Allen
YOUNG SOLDIER IN PARK	Greg Cruttwell
FIRST LADY	Annie Hayes
FIRST DUTCH YOUTH	Nicholas Teare
YOUNG OFFICER	Wayne Foskett
POLICEMAN	Philip Bretherton
RECEPTIONIST	Eric Allan
BLONDE WOMAN	Eileen Maciejewska
PRISONER	Will Tacey
SERGEANT	Neale McGrath
SS COLONEL	Richard Cubison
BUILDER	Arthur Whybrow
BROWNSHIRT AT SYNAGOGUE	David Bauckham
FREDA	Barbara Marten
JACOB	Frank Baker

PRIEST	Robert Howard
SECOND DUTCH YOUTH	Mark Draper
THIRD DUTCH YOUTH	Tom Lambert
FOURTH DUTCH YOUTH	Simon Adams
IRATE WOMAN IN RUBBLE	Joolia Cappleman
CLARITA	Nicola Wright
SECOND LADY	Tricia Kelly
THIRD LADY	Maureen Bennett
CLERK	Wilfrid Grove
FAT BROWNSHIRT	Stewart Harwood
FIRST NAZI	John Phythian
SECOND NAZI	Tim Killick
UNDERMANAGER AT HOTEL	Michael Egan
FIRST MEMBER OF ENGLAND COMMITTEE	Paul Kiernan
SECOND MEMBER	Louis Mellis
OLDER MEMBER	Roy Heather
FIRST SOLDIER ON TRAIN	Kim Kindersley
SECOND SOLDIER	Paul M. Meston
THIRD SOLDIER	Duncan Piney
GESTAPO DRIVER	Simon Tyrrell
FIRST SS OFFICER	John Gillett
SECOND SS OFFICER	Christopher Leaver
ALOIS	John Boswall
YOUNG MAN AT CINEMA	Grant Parsons
POW AT STATION	Wayne Norman
SHOPKEEPER	John Barrard
NEWSVENDOR	Jonathan Izard
GUARD	Ian Lowe
GERMAN TEACHER	Sue Withers
SOLDIER	Danny McCarthy

Children

NICKY	James Stewart, Sam Preston, Toby Lawson, Alastair Haley
JOHN	Ben Preston, Ryan Le Neveu, Andrey Justice, James Exell

EDELTRAUT	Emma-Louise Harrington
HILDE	Laura Goodwin
BOY SOLDIER	Lawrence Cooper
ILSE's SON	Oliver Taylor-Medhurst
Make-up	Deanne Turner
Costume	Anushia Nieradzik
Sound	Peter Edwards
Lighting Cameraman	Remi Adefarasin
Film Editor	Clare Douglas
Designer	Jim Clay
Executive Producer	Dennis Potter
Producer	Kenith Trodd
Director	Adrian Shergold

Note: This text includes some scenes and passages of dialogue which were cut during the editing process and do not appear in the transmitted version.

ONE

England, 1934. A mellow old house basking in the sunshine of an idyllic September morning, serene within its own green acres. We approach through a cluster of grand trees, across a paddock where sleek horses crop, past the round pond with its flotilla of ducks. This slow and stately approach is one that seems to understand or even relish the mood of wealth, ease and tranquillity.

Fading in, on the move, the seemingly distant, faintly scratched, sweetly wistful and yet somehow oddly threatening 78–r.p.m. record of Annette Hanshaw singing 'I'm Following You'.

Several gleaming Rolls-Royces, 1930s vintage, are parked on the gravel, circular drive in front of the house. They are decorated with silk ribbons, for a wedding. Uniformed chauffeurs stand together, talking and smoking. One of them laughs, and looks up at the house.

The music is coming from one of the upper-floor windows, which are opened wide to the bright morning sun.

Inside, Christabel, a beauty in her early twenties, is studying herself with calm self-possession in a long mirror, deciding where, or whether, to pin a sprig of lavender on her flowing white wedding dress. But she is also more than half-listening to the music, which comes from an old wind-up gramophone near to the open window.
CHRISTOBEL: (*To herself, faint smile*) That's absolutely right.

On the wide stairs outside, Christabel's father, Mr Burton, attired in formal morning dress for the wedding, sits alone on one of the steps, his grey top hat on his knees. The song on the gramophone spills down the stairs.

His whole posture is that of a deeply troubled or even alienated man, staring straight ahead at nothing but his own thoughts.

At the top of the stair, where the gramophone music is louder, Christabel's mother, Mrs Burton, hestiates at Christabel's door, seems to take a deep breath, taps on the door, and opens it.

There is now a growing sense that something is wrong, or mysteriously out of place in what should be the happy mood of a wedding day morning.

Christabel turns to smile at the opening door. But her smile falters a little at the strained expression on her mother's face.

CHRISTABEL: (*Wry*) Well, Mother. 'Something old, and something new –' Will I do?

MRS BURTON: Christabel. Oh, Christabel.

Christabel sees that the tears are about to brim. Mysteriously, they are of anxiety, it seems, and not joy.

CHRISTABEL: Now, now! What's this? Face as long as a fiddle!

MRS BURTON: My dear. You can have no idea of how – heartbreakingly lovely you look at this moment.

CHRISTABEL: (*Deliberately pert*) Oh yes I do! I've been studying myself in the mirror. And it didn't splinter!

MRS BURTON: I just wish – I just wish you –

CHRISTABEL: (*Interrupting*) Don't. Please. You mustn't spoil things for me.

MRS BURTON: But I can't bear to think of what might happen to you –

She is twisting her hands. We must wonder what is wrong, what is the mystery spoiling this peaceful house, sunlit morning, and threatening such a lovely young bride . . .

Almost ominously, the music begins to slur and distort as the gramophone winds down.

Christabel is clearly glad of the diversion. She winds the handle of the gramophone, vigorously. The music picks up again, and regains the right tempo.

CHRISTABEL: Oh, nothing can happen to *me*, Mother – (*Laugh.*) Don't you just love this silly little tune?

MRS BURTON: Christabel –

CHRISTABEL: It's been humming in my head for days now.

MRS BURTON: (*Doggedly*) Christabel. The fact that Peter went to Oxford is no guarantee that he'll always see things in the same way that *you've* been brought up to see them –

CHRISTABEL: Mother.

MRS BURTON: You know we like Peter, and we have the greatest possible respect for him – of course we do –

CHRISTABEL: (*Dismissing all this*) I think I'll take this silly old song

2

with me. I'll bet you I'll break it though!

They look at each other. Each, mysteriously, seems to be silently imploring the other. The Annette Hanshaw vocal returns on the record.

MRS BURTON: Christabel. Don't you have *any* premonitions?

The vocal carries through on Christabel's dismissive but kindly meant laugh to where –

Respectful villagers are clustering outside the ancient village church, eager to see all the comings and goings for the local Wedding of the Year. There is a murmur of interest and a certain discreet pressing foward as two young men get out of a newly arrived limousine. They are the groom, Peter Bielenberg, and his friend, later to be identified as Adam von Trott.

Peter and Adam – out of earshot – exchange some light remark, and Peter laughs as they pass into the church. But some of the spectators are staring at them with more than usually intense interest: by no means unfriendly, and yet distinctly without the expected warmth.

As the song fades, the church bells reassert themselves in a joyous bing–bang–bong.

The now distant bells come across the meadows and hedgerows, mingled with bird song.

A beribboned Rolls is pulled up at the side of the road, by a grassy bank. The chauffeur sits at the wheel, very overtly minding his own business.

Beyond the waiting car, Christabel and her father stand by a farm gate, which yields a vista of fields and stream and the distant spire of the village church.

MR BURTON: (*Spreading arm*) Look at it. All of it! What do you see? Eh?

She is a distracted and reluctant sightseer, who has to hitch up her wedding dress to stop it trailing in the long grass.

CHRISTABEL: Grass.

MR BURTON: (*Irritated*) What *sort* of grass – ?

CHRISTABEL: Green grass.

She laughs – and he explodes.

MR BURTON: I'm sorry, my girl – but if you think this is an occasion

3

for levity then I have to tell you we do not see eye to eye! Not one bit!

CHRISTABEL: Oh. Crikey.

MR BURTON: It's English grass, Christabel – *English* grass!

CHRISTABEL: Oh. Yes. Yes, of course.

She wants to laugh. He controls himself.

MR BURTON: All around you, Christabel. Look at it. Think! Your own, your dear, your native land –

CHRISTABEL: (*Sigh.*) Father –

MR BURTON: And in each and every village of it you'll find a plaque or a statue or a cross of stone –

CHRISTABEL: Can't you hear the bells – !

MR BURTON: (*Sweeping on*) A war memorial, Christabel – to those who fell, my girl. Defending us!

Christabel turns away, exasperated, still hitching up her flowing white dress.

CHRISTABEL: I'm *not* going to miss my own wedding, Father.

MR BURTON: Who from? Eh? Defending us against what? Who were they – eh?

The chauffeur is getting out of the Rolls, to help Christabel in.

CHRISTABEL: Hawkins – do we hit him on the head, or go without him?

But Mr Burton is making a loud and anguished appeal.

MR BURTON: It's not too late to back out of it, Christabel! All we have to do is turn this damned wagon around – Just give the word – eh?

In the village church, full to the doors for the big occasion.

PRIEST: – Therefore if any man can show any just cause why they may not lawfully be joined together, let him now speak – (*Settling on Christabel's father*) – or else hereafter for ever hold his peace.

Mr Burton twitches, comically: but that is all.

> Peter. Wilt thou have this woman to thy wedded wife, to live together after God's ordinance in the holy estate of matrimony? Wilt thou love her, comfort her, honour, and keep her, in sickness and in health, and, forsaking all other, keep thee only unto her, so long as ye both shall live?

A small beat, taking relevant faces, then –

4

PETER: Ja, mit Gottes Hilfe.
A discernible tremor of surprise, all round. Then the groom gives a
slight bow of the head, and a little smile.
        I will.
Bells ring, ring, become silent, and then – blackness.

Gradually coming out of the blackness into a silvered moonlight, a
gigantic Nazi banner seems to sigh and to whisper as its silk
brushes and shifts against the building stone.

Banners and flags are draped in row upon row on the massive
public buildings. There is a long and slowly darkening perspective
of swastikas. In the moonlight, at the dead of night, with nobody in
sight, and the flags flap–flap–flapping, it feels ominously
expectant. Almost simultaneously, comes the distant rumble from
many streets away of armoured vehicles in convoy.

The trucks, packed full of German troops in steel helmets, thunder
through the empty night streets.

Truck upon truck, armoured carrier upon armoured carrier,
swirling past in convoy, shattering the night, bouncing back its
own sounds in the darkly cavernous street.
        It is Berlin. March, 1938.

In the hall of Christabel's new home in Berlin, a few lead soldiers
are out of a toybox in the corner of the hall. It is night-time.
        Above them, the throaty Tick–h Tock–h of a cased clock, in
which the pendulum swings and glints and swings. A silvery chime
strikes three in the morning.

In her bedroom, Christabel is awake, and hears the chimes die
away, from the hall below. Christabel is lying very still in bed, in
the half-light, seemingly turning things over in her mind. Then she
turns to look at Peter, apparently fast asleep in the adjoining bed.
CHRISTABEL: (*Whisper*) Peter – ?
No reply. A moment. Then –
        (*Thinks*) What is going to happen? What are we going to do?
A moment. Then she quietly slips out of bed, and, in her

5

nightgown, barefoot, goes to the door. As she softly opens it, a diagonal of light widens, and as it falls across Peter's bed it becomes clear that he is not, after all, asleep. The closing door narrows the light again, but not before revealing the troubled, brooding expression in his eyes.

Christabel, peeping in at the children's bedroom, sees her first-born, Nicholas, not yet three, curled up asleep, clutching a toy red London bus. His younger brother, John, is also asleep in his cot, uncovered. Christabel gently covers him over again, and looks at them both, her small smile again becoming thoughtful.

As Christabel closes the door upon the sleeping children, she realizes – with a slight start – that Peter is standing there, watching her. They look at each other, silently, then –

PETER: (*Whisper*) All right?

CHRISTABEL: (*Whisper*) Fast asleep.

They hold their gaze at each other. Then –

PETER: Round and round and round. The same thoughts in the same old way. Stay. Go. Go. Stay. They're asleep. Are *we* asleep?

CHRISTABEL: I don't know.

A moment. Then they seem suddenly propelled towards one another, and they embrace.

In the Berlin streets beyond, the military convoy continues to thunder menacingly, apparently endlessly. Part of some big new political fact –

The next morning or so, an excited newsvendor with a First World War ribbon on his patched jacket is shouting the big news, shrill and insistent.

VENDOR: Achtung! – Achtung! Extrablatt – Extrablatt! Die deutschen Truppen sind in Osterreich einmarschiert! Die deutschen Truppen sind in Osterreich einmarschiert! Achtung! – Achtung –!

Beneath the fat, flag-decked buildings, people are hurrying to buy extra-edition newspapers. They grab for the papers, quickly read, and gather together in voluble groups, excited, even festive.

In the doctor's consulting room, the newsvendor's now distant cries are only just audible through the partly opened window of this upper-floor room much further down the street.

Even so, Professor Bauer, a paediatrician, reacts to it, closing the window, and turning back into the room with the half-apologetic smile of an old and tired man.

BAUER: Noise.

CHRISTABEL: What *is* that fellow shouting –? There seems to be something going on –

She is with her small son, Nicholas. Bauer appears to change his mind about what he is about to say, like a man who has learnt caution.

BAUER: Always there is something going on, Frau Bielenberg. You may put your tongue away, Nicky. It is so nice and pink that it must go back into its own warm little cupboard.

NICKY: (*Delighted*) Yeth! Cupboard – !

Immediately dropping on to his knees to push the toy London bus up and down, with suitable bus noises.

CHRISTABEL: He slept like a log last night – (*Laughs.*) So of course I didn't. But the rash seems to have all cleared up. I'm glad it wasn't anything serious.

BAUER: (*Severely*) All childhood ailments are serious.

CHRISTABEL: Oh, come now –

But Bauer interrupts her, abrupt, even rude.

BAUER: Frau Bielenberg. Do you still wish me to attend your children? Does you husband?

Christabel, misunderstanding, is astonished.

CHRISTABEL: What? Why ever not? Have I offended you in some –

BAUER: Frau Bielenberg. I am a Jew.

CHRISTABEL: Oh. Are you?

Said with such so-what? indifference or naïvety that it is his turn to be astonished.

BAUER: Your husband is – Dr Bielenberg. He is a lawyer.

CHRISTABEL: Yes. But – ?

BAUER: (*Severe*) In a single-party state, Frau Doktor, the law is – (*He gives up, exasperated.*) Are you pretending you do not understand?

CHRISTABEL: If you are talking politics, count me out, Professor Bauer.

BAUER: (*Sigh*) Frau Bielenberg –

CHRISTABEL: (*Patrician English*) Now look here – What on earth has this got to do with chickenpox! I don't want to be rude, but what has your religion got to do with it?

He spreads his hands in mock despair, almost amused.

BAUER: Frau Bielenberg. You speak German very well. I would say faultlessly except – My dear lady. What you actually *say* is very very English.

CHRISTABEL: Oh? But I still don't –

BAUER: (*Interrupting*) I have been warned in no uncertain terms not to treat Aryan children.

Vroom! Vroom! from Nicky, with his toy, obtrusively. Christabel looks at him, and then, taking it in, back at Bauer.

CHRISTABEL: But that's – oh, now, this is preposterous.

He smiles an old and tired smile.

BAUER: More precisely, my dear, to keep my dirty Jew hands off them. I do not wish trouble for you. For your husband.

In the street below, the same newsvendor, same shrill cry of excitement, but now heard in English.

VENDOR: News Extra! Extra! Extra! German Troops march into Austria! Extra! News Extra! –

Christabel, holding Nicky's hand, comes into view, looking at the excited vendor who is selling papers as fast as he can, with unmodulated cries.

She half hesitates, as though to get a paper too. Then turns away, decisively, with a frown.

In the living room of the Bielenberg house, during the evening, the grating rant of Adolf Hitler coming from a fluted and whorled 1930s radio.

Listening, sprawled in after-dinner postures, are Peter and his friend and contemporary Adam von Trott. Their eyes slowly settle on each other as the Hitler speech surges around them. They say nothing.

Upstairs, in the children's bedroom, Christabel is quietly singing and humming to the toddler John, who is reluctantly eyelid-drooping into sleep on the cot. Nicholas appears to be asleep in his bed.

CHRISTABEL: (*Softly sings*) – Five men went to mow, Went to mow
     a meadow, Five men – four men – three men – two men – one
     man and his dog – Went to mow a –
NICKY: (*Suddenly*) No more mowing!
CHRISTABEL: Sssh. John's asleep now.
John's eyes have indeed closed. Christabel goes to Nicky, kisses
him.
     And you, too. Sleepy bye-byes. Night-night.
He settles down. She goes to the door. As it opens –
NICKY: (*Suddenly*) Mummy. What is a Jew?

Downstairs, the radio is still belching out Hitlerian rhetoric, and
the two men still look silently at each other.

Christabel comes from the stair, past the throaty clock, towards the
living room, from which the Hitler radio speech can be heard.
     She frowns at the noise, and glances back at the stairs.

Adam, moving at last, is helping himself to brandy as an annoyed
Christabel enters.
CHRISTABEL: Isn't this a bit loud? I've just got them quiet
     upstairs –
ADAM: You mean, you want to put *this* infant to sleep too?
CHRISTABEL: Not with a lullaby!
Adam puts his hand on the radio switch, and mimics the tones of a
stage magician.
ADAM: Lad–eez and Gentle–men! I, Adam von Trott zu Solz cast
     out this malignant hobgoblin! I condemn him to utter
     darkness and –
CHRISTABEL: (*Laugh*) Eternal silence!
ADAM: – and eternal Silence – Yes! Ab–ra–cad–ab–*ra*!
Click! the still-ranting Hitler is silenced in mid-word. Boyish
Adam laughs, as does Christabel.
     But Peter has remained ominously quiet. He has not raised even
a ghost of a smile.
PETER: But we can't, can we, Adam? You're not the sorcerer. He is.
ADAM: I can turn him *off*.
PETER: But it's not just a voice, is it? And it's there all the time.
     You can't really turn it off. Can you?

9

ADAM: (*Bluntly*) All right. Then what exactly do you propose to do about it?

Christabel looks carefully from one to the other, sensing challenge.

PETER: Perhaps there is nothing we *can* do. How do we know it is not already too late? Past the point of any possible return?

ADAM: Don't say that!

PETER: Perhaps all we can do is compromise and eventually corrupt ourselves.

ADAM: No!

PETER: A small concession here. Another one there. Bit by bit. Until we are trapped. Physically and morally.

ADAM: (*Subdued*) No.

CHRISTABEL: (*Suddenly*) We can leave.

PETER: Precisely.

ADAM: *No! No! No!*

PETER: *Yes! Yes! Yes!*

The two exchanges zip out like sudden and unexpected explosions. Each man registers the other's swift passion with a blink of surprise. A beat of tension. Then –

CHRISTABEL: Who would like coffee?

But neither at this moment has eyes or ears for her.

PETER: You're not married, Adam. You don't have any children to think about –

ADAM: All children! All the children in Germany!

CHRISTABEL: Adam. I took Nicky to the doctor the other day. The sweetest man. And, do you know, he –

ADAM: (*Interrupting*) We have to stop them before it's too late!

PETER: But, Adam – isn't that just wishful thinking? The Germany we wanted and hoped for – Pffutt!

ADAM: (*Hotly*) You're saying it's already gone. Smashed to pieces. Totally beyond repair?

A small, but distinctly measured and weighted pause.

PETER: Yes.

ADAM: With no hope at all?

Christabel's eyes are now fixed on Peter. She can see his reluctance, even though he speaks with quiet deliberation.

PETER: Yes. That is what I am saying. The truth.

Adam makes a violent gesture.

CHRISTABEL: Adam. I love this country. Four years nearly I've

spent here since I married Peter. They've been quite literally
the happiest of my life –

ADAM: Well, then!

CHRISTABEL: But even I can see how things are going – and I'm the
least political person you'll ever – (*Her voice changes.*) Adam.
There are two small children fast asleep upstairs. Can Peter
and I risk letting them wake up into a – a – nightmare?

Adam stares down into his glass, twirling it unhappily.

Later, outside: a tree-lined street of solid old houses, in which
Peter is accompanying Adam to his car. Adam looks about, then –
quietly –

ADAM: Listen to me. It *will* be a nightmare if people like us allow it
to happen –

PETER: People like us?

ADAM: Why do you think I've got myself an attachment to the
Foreign Office?

PETER: Adam –

ADAM: (*A little too loudly*) And why do you imagine there are not
hundreds of others like me – ? Thousands, Peter. Tens of
thousands – !

But his voice suddenly drops. A man passes, walking his dog. They
watch him go. Then –

PETER: (*Quietly*) Thousands. Tens of thousands.

ADAM: Yes!

PETER: And what are they doing? Whispering? Looking up and
down at their own front door? In case a man and his dog
should pass by.

Adam stares at him, then turns abruptly away, to go to his car.

ADAM: Good night.

Peter watches him go, troubled. Adam opens his car door,
immediately under the orange glow of an elderly street light.

PETER: (*Half calls*) Adam. I want to believe you. I *want* to!

Adam shuts the car door, walks back, looks closely at Peter, almost
unnervingly so. And then – with a quiet, measured intensity –

ADAM: You and I both agreed that we would not take the Oath of
Loyalty to the Führer. We swore on it.

PETER: (*Solemn*) We did.

ADAM: That makes us comrades. Doesn't it?

A beat. Peter looks at the upstairs window of his house, then steadily back at Adam.

PETER: What do you want me to do?

Adam nods, satisfied. And then, mock conspiratorial, raises his fingers to his lips, in an exaggerated 'Shhh!' gesture, and smiles a brilliant smile.

Day, again. A slow, simple-faced but kindly looking Saxon, Neisse, a jobbing gardener, is busy clip–clip–clip with his shears at shrub and bush in the large old garden. His tongue out in concentration.

CHRISTABEL: Goodness, Herr Neisse. Those thorns! Shouldn't
    you be wearing gloves?

Her sudden appearance rather startles him. She is bearing a steaming mug of coffee. Neisse springs up from a low stoop at the thicket of blackthorn, polite, flustered.

NEISSE: Frau Bielenberg! Good day!

CHRISTABEL: If you're not careful, you'll tear yourself to bits.

NEISSE: Oh, mind, Frau Bielenberg – the little old birds d'like 'em,
    mind, these here thorns. Ooh, aye. For their little old nests,
    y'see. Safe as houses – (*Disconcerting cackle*.) Excepting for the
    likes of I!

CHRISTABEL: (*Amused*) There was supposed to be a nightingale in
    this garden.

NEISSE: Ooh. Was there, now?

CHRISTABEL: Well, that's what we were told when we bought the
    house – but I've never heard it. Wu–u–u! Isn't this wind
    chilly! I've brought you some hot coffee.

NEISSE: Oh, very nice, very kind. Ay – a cold old March like this –
    Don't you stay out here. It goes right through you, this wind.
    Ay – We don't call it spring, we Saxon folk don't, a-wittering
    and a-blowing like this!

She tries not to laugh at his slow solemnity.

CHRISTABEL: Don't we?

NEISSE: Nooo, we don't. We'd a call it a blackthorn winter – See –
    when thee's get these here little white flowers on the thorn –

CHRISTABEL: Oh – aren't they pretty!

But she also shivers.

NEISSE: Ay! They show their little faces in the east wind, y'see.

Always a cold easterly wi' these little devils. (*Disconcerting cackle again.*) But by God we shall have us some real sun to warm our bones *this* time!

CHRISTABEL: (*Smile*) You think so?

NEISSE: You've heard the good tidings, eh?

She looks at him. There is a different glint in his eye. Her expression changes.

CHRISTABEL: Is there any?

NEISSE: The Anschluss!

CHRISTABEL: Oh. Yes.

His own pleasure too great for him to notice her lack of enthusiasm.

NEISSE: We be one land now. Germany and Austria. One people. One leader. Ay – we got us the right man in charge now, ant us? (*The disconcerting cackle.*) All is lovely in the garden, Frau Bielenberg!

Her expression hardens.

CHRISTABEL: Are you talking about the blossom, or the thorns?

Neisse, puzzled by any verbal complication, stares after her as she abruptly turns back to the house. Then his face splits in another odd cackle.

NEISSE: Ah – but we shall *burn* the thorns! Cut 'em down! Set light to 'em! We got us a good gardener now, Frau Bielenberg!

Night and the city. The Brownshirts are out with their torches.

Crude, anti-Semitic slogans scrawled on doors and walls, and crash! as a window caves in.

A mob of cheering Nazis breaks down the window with sledge-hammers, buckling the protective grille behind the shattered glass.

Raucous cheering from the Brownshirts, as they pull out the goods to be scattered on the pavement, to be spat and trampled on.

In the ballroom of an elegant Berlin hotel, on that same evening, a dinner-jacket dance band bounces out a fox-trot, and elegant couples swirl on a polished floor, beneath alabaster cupids.

Finding, amongst them, Christabel and Peter – and Peter's distracted awkwardness.

CHRISTABEL: Ow – !

13

PETER: Oops. Sorry.
He has stepped on her toe – and not for the first time.
CHRISTABEL: Why didn't you say you'd rather be playing
football – ?
PETER: (*Abstracted*) What?
CHRISTABEL: Peter!
PETER: Sorry – sorry – I'm one of those oafs who can't think and
dance at the same time.
CHRISTABEL: What about *talking* and dancing?
PETER: Yes?
CHRISTABEL: (*Laugh*) Where are you, Peter? What is the matter?
He stops dancing, and looks at her, serious.

Outside, at the same time, rampaging Brownshirts, leaving
another smashed shop, surge out of a side street into the broad and
brightly lit main thoroughfare.
   Running for dear life in front of them is a terrified man, his shirt
torn. He is not fast enough for the predominantly youthful
pursuers.
   He is cornered at the high windows of the hotel, and
systematically beaten to the ground, with accompanying cheers.

Inside the hotel, an art-deco nook of glass and chrome, semi-
private, in which Peter and Christabel are at a table small enough
for knee-collision. They have drinks.
PETER: Some night out for you! Bruised feet and a brooding
partner. You'd have had more fun in the kitchen.
The dance band can be heard – or even partially seen – beyond the
glass fluting of the alcove.
CHRISTABEL: (*Laugh*) Oh – I'd as soon get squiffy! (*At his non-
response*) Peter. What is it?
PETER: Christabel. I love you.
His tone makes her nervous.
CHRISTABEL: I love you too.
PETER: I still – something still jumps inside me when I – (*Sudden
change.*) Christabel. Rain or shine. Near or far.
CHRISTABEL: Something's wrong. I can see. Something has
happened.
PETER: (*Steadily*) I think you should go home to England.

14

CHRISTABEL: (*Tensing*) Me? Don't you mean we – ?

PETER: Christabel. Bad things are happening here. You know
   that –

CHRISTABEL: We. You mean *us*.

PETER: – And far, far worse things are going to happen –

CHRISTABEL: Us. Both! You mean *both*!

PETER: Christabel. Listen.

CHRISTABEL: No!

PETER: This afternoon, I –

CHRISTABEL: You've been meeting Adam and his friends, haven't
   you? (*Rising tone*) What have *we* got to do with politics – that
   stuff! – I am not leaving. Not without you.

He puts his hands very firmly on hers, across the table.

His quiet intensity makes her stare, yet also calm down.

The dance band plays on.

PETER: This afternoon, in court, I defended an old Social
   Democrat who had been – (*Gesture of disgust*) He'd been
   handing out leaflets. Which is now a crime.

CHRISTABEL: (*Grimly*) Go on. What happened?

But he surprises her.

PETER: No. The Court actually-decided-to-let-him-go. (*Bitterly*)
   Oh. I was so full of myself. Very proud of my eloquence.

CHRISTABEL: (*Puzzled*) Peter?

PETER: We pumped each other's hands. We practically embraced
   each other. Oh, oh, it's a wonderful feeling to think that the law
   still means something above and beyond the will of the Party –

In Peter's mind, flying back to the Court House, two policemen
skulk out from behind stone pillars as Peter and an old man – the
Social Democrat – come happily down the wide, long stone steps
towards the pavement.

   Peter and his released client shake hands vigorously, on the
pavement, unaware of the watching police. The triumphant old
man slaps him on the shoulder, says something, Peter grins, and
they go off in opposite directions.

   Peter strides away, exuberant, energetic. But a shout makes him
stop and turn, to see –

   The two policemen are violently hauling the struggling Social

Democrat towards a green van, parked further along the street.

Peter runs towards them, yelling.

PETER: Hey – ! No! Stop!

The police cuff the old man into a limp bundle as the back doors of the van swing open from inside. They throw him in, like a sack of potatoes.

Peter gets there as the van doors are slammed shut. He hammers on the back of the van and tries to hold on – unavailingly – as it rapidly accelerates away.

Bystanders, watching, immobile, turn away, furtive, embarrassed, or worried.

PETER: (*Yell*) Did you see that? Did you see what happened!

But they don't want to know.

In the hotel bar, Christabel offers inadequate comfort.

CHRISTABEL: It's not because they are evil or because they – It's because they're frightened or – What can they actually *do*? I mean . . .

But her voice trails off at the pain in his eyes.

PETER: All afternoon I spent at the Law Courts and at the Police Headquarters and – No, no, Doktor Bielenberg – No, no, Herr Doktor – you must be mistaken – Doktor Bielenberg, what are you talking about? No, no, no!

His mimicry has been too savage. He is all but trembling with a dangerously pent-in rage. She reaches across to put her hands over his fists as they clench on the table.

CHRISTABEL: Let's go home.

PETER: (*Hardly listening*) Fill in this form. Fill in that form. *What is the matter with you? Why are you doing this?* That's what they say. Or that's what they mean. All those quiet, respectable officials of the law. *Don't!* they say *Don't involve me.* Sshhh! Sshh! Tread softly, young man. Be sensible. *Why do this?*

He looks at Christabel, like one suddenly emptied of all spirit. Exhausted.

CHRISTABEL: I'm sorry. I'm very sorry.

PETER: Why *am* I doing it? For what? How *can* one continue as a lawyer when there is no law? Christabel. This is it. I am not going to be a performing monkey in the Court House. I have to stop. I must – *must* stop.

CHRISTABEL: (*Firmly*) Then, yes, we have to leave. Both of us.
Together. Get out of Germany. The time for talking about it is over.
PETER: Christabel. I – Listen. Darling. Adam can get me into the
Foreign Office, and it's still not too late to –
He stops, as both of them become aware of a commotion in the big,
elegant bar beyond. Swaggering Brownshirts are swarming in from
the street, pleased with themselves, shouting for beer.
Bastards. Oh, the bastards!
Christabel sees the way his hand tightens claw-like on his glass.
CHRISTABEL: (*Urgently*) Careful.

A respectful but anxiously smiling undermanager intervenes as the
Berlin socialites in the bar look askance at the mostly young
roughnecks.
UNDERMANAGER: Gentlemen – Gentlemen – ! Please – ! A little
more decorum!
The noise level falls off momentarily. But then –
FAT BROWNSHIRT: Up your arse, lackey!
Raucous laughter from many (not all) of the Nazis. Some of them
look uneasy or even embarrassed.

Peter throws some money on to the table, in disgust.
PETER: So much for our night out. Come on. Let's go. Let's get
away from the whole damn lot of it!
Beyond, the Nazi 'Horst Wessel Song' breaks out, bellowing from
one end of the long bar, and many of the guests do not like it.
A thunderous-faced Peter leads Christabel through the
crowding Nazis. Others, too, are deciding to get out, including a
uniformed Wehrmacht officer and his lady.
The fat Nazi is so eager to join the group of singers that he steps
back heavily and clumsily on to Peter's foot. Pain releases Peter's
pent-in rage and humiliation. With a hard, open-palmed shove on
the chest, the fat Nazi – helped by his own weight – is sent hurtling
backwards – crash! – very hard against bar stools and some of his
companions to end flat on his back.
A startled shock of silence. Even the singing stops.
Peter looks down at the sprawled, gaping figure, speaking at first
with cold formality, apparently polite.

17

May I point out that it is considered impolite to walk on other people. But you have no means of knowing that. You are an ignorant oaf.

With which, holding Christabel's hand, he turns briskly away to the revolving doors of the exist, the fallen man gaping at him, comically. A sudden roar of laughter.

JEERING VOICES: Oaf! Oaf! Who's an oaf!

But, then, Peter's coldly imperious contempt, as suddenly, sinks in, helped by the reaction of the non-Nazis in the bar.

FIRST NAZI: Who the shit does he think he is!

SECOND NAZI: Is that respect? Do you call *that* respect – ?

VOICES: Respect! Respect!

An ugly chorus, and some of them go after Peter –

Crashing out of the revolving doors, some of the Nazis look up and down the wide, well-lit pavements for Peter and Christabel.

Fortunately, there is a throng of passers-by, coming from a near-by cinema, and although they are given a discreetly wide berth, the Brownshirts eventually see Christabel and Peter getting into their parked car – and noisily career after them.

The leading Brownshirts catch up with the car as it is about to drive off.

Moving away, into the stream of traffic, Peter's car is attacked, the Brownshirts banging on the door and on the roof of the car, shouting obscenities, and yet also grinning as though it were not of the ultimate importance.

The car, accelerating into the main flow, soon loses its assailants.

Into freer flow of traffic, away from the centre, Peter's eyes blaze, and his jaw is set, as he drives. He seems to be unaware of Christabel's concerned but eventually sardonic examination. An Anglo-German question, so to speak.

CHRISTABEL: What a lot of fuss. Just because someone stepped on *your* toes. Mmm?

PETER: (*Angry*) It wasn't the way he – (*A beat. He gets the joke about his dancing.*) I see. I see. Don't you try your British sarcasm on me, my love – or I'll never dance with you again.

CHRISTABEL: You promise?

He looks sideways at her. She pouts her lips in a pretend kiss.

PETER: (*Relaxing*) Do you want to drop off somewhere else –
    another drink, or – ?

CHRISTABEL: And meet more gorillas?

PETER: No, no.

CHRISTABEL: What about our baby-sitter? I've the feeling he'll be
    glad to see us back early.

PETER: (*Airily*) Oh, Adam can cope. He's a very capable person.

A sudden dazzle of flashlight and a worried Adam von Trott, in the
garden of the Bielenberg house.

ADAM: Nicky! Where are you? Nicky! Please! (*Sterner*) Nicholas.
    Answer me at once! (*Quavering*) Come on. There's a good lad
    . . . *Please* – (*A desperate mutter*) O God. Oh, my God . . .

And he hears, from back in the house –

Toddler John, waking and finding himself alone, stands in his cot,
fists gripping the wooden bars, howls, bereft.

In the car, returning home, Peter brakes sharply.

PETER: What the – !

They have reached a poorly lit, shabbier area of the city. A large,
silent crowd overfills the narrow pavement, opposite a fast-burning
building.

    A Brownshirt has suddenly stepped out, arm raised, to make
Peter's car stop so sharply.

Peter winds down his window.

PETER: What is it? What's going on?

BROWNSHIRT: Never you mind. You'll have to back out of here.
    Come on!

PETER: What do you mean? Who do you think you're talking to?

The Brownshirt is a little taken aback by the imperiousness of
Peter's manner. He eyes Peter, reluctantly uncertain.

BROWNSHIRT: It's the Jew House.

PETER: What? What do you mean?

BROWNSHIRT: (*Spits.*) Synagogue.

CHRISTABEL: No!

PETER: Where are the police? Where's the fire brigade? Why aren't
they here – !
He tries to open the car door. The Brownshirt pushes against it.
Others in brown are also gathering around, not friendly.
You can't do this! What right have you to – Let me out!

Christabel stares ahead, frozen, at –

A cascade of sparks shoots up, and then huge tongues of flame, as
the upper part of the building collapses inward.
Lit by crackling flame, the staring, upturned faces of the
watchers seem oddly devoid of almost any emotion, like people
standing by in the middle of someone's bad dream.
Only a relatively few are grinning or gesticulating with obvious
delight. The rest seem unable to react at all.
We hear again the same wistfully threatening little song as at the
beginning: 'I'm Following You', the words buckling under the
weight of new meaning.

As the song swells in her mind, and flames reflect in the car, and in
her eyes, Christabel is drained of both anger and alarm. She speaks
in a flat dead voice.
CHRISTABEL: Take me home. Peter. I want my children. I want to
hold my children.
He looks at her, upset, then nods, as though to himself, and
reverses the car, slowly, through the press of people.

In the street, silhouetted onlookers against the flame and smoke.
An evil chiaroscuro of faces and fire.

Dark streets scud by, through the car windows. Christabel, sad
and brooding, is locked into herself. She eventually looks out, and
sees –

A long, high hoarding, half the length of a street, plastered with
picture after picture of Adolf Hitler, with slogans and swastikas,
almost in rhythmic sequence to the song that still sounds in her
mind, its meanings now subverted.

The music dies on Christabel's face as she turns to look at Peter, and at last speaks. They have arrived home.

CHRISTABEL: Why? *Why?*

Then she seems to hunch into herself, staring down at her hands on her lap. Peter, switching off the ignition, looks at her with concern.

PETER: Christabel.

CHRISTABEL: (*Suddenly, savagely*) I cannot even begin to
    understand! What sort of people are you!

PETER: Me? Do you mean? *Me* . . . ?

She makes a sound in her throat.

    (*Steadily*) You must leave this place. You must go back to
    England. (*Small trace of bitterness.*) The lucky land.

CHRISTABEL: And you? Peter – ?

PETER: I must stay. It is my duty.

They hold glances, examining each other.

Then, like a swift premonition of personal grief, something snaps inside her. She draws in her breath sharply, jerks open the car door and runs towards the house.

Peter sighs, then slaps his hands hard on the steering wheel, just once, in distress.

As Christabel bursts into the hall, upset, Adam is coming down the stairs, within her view. He stops, and looks down at her, a picture of woe.

ADAM: (*Croak*) Christabel.

His forehead is cut, his eye bruised. Her face changes, fearing for her children.

CHRISTABEL: Adam! What has happened – !

ADAM: (*Forlorn*) I have just had the worst experience of my entire
    life.

CHRISTABEL: Is it the children – !

ADAM: The children.

He does not, of course, know the state she is in, and had intended to be comically lugubrious. But she is racing up the stairs, past him, as Peter comes in to the hall.

    (*Startled*) No – no! *They're* all right –

PETER: What is it?

ADAM: (*To Peter*) Christ. It's *me* that needs attention. Where do
    you keep the brandy?

PETER: What have you done to your face . . . ?
Adam spreads his hands in rueful apology.
ADAM: Hide and seek. Hide and bloody seek.

Later, in the living room, Peter and Christabel listen with amused
incredulity.
ADAM: I tell you – I thought something dreadful must have
    happened. I thought the little monster had gone for good.
PETER: But the toolshed was the *obvious* place –
ADAM: I looked in the toolshed. I looked all over the damned
    toolshed. Twice! No sight. No sound. The little monster had
    literally *covered* himself with the wheelbarrow. And would he
    answer? Not a peep! That's when I stepped on the rake. It
    leapt up like mad thing and sunk its teeth into me! (*As they
    laugh*) God – the pain! – And then the other little bugger woke
    up – *Waa! Waaaa!* – Is that me, I thought. Is that *me* crying?
    Never again. Never. Never. Never!
Christabel and Peter are laughing – but her laughter has the edge of
distress, and, just as Adam belatedly realizes it, she puts her hands
to her face, deeply upset.
    Oh. But I –
Peter crosses to her, quickly, as she begins to weep, to put his arms
around her.
PETER: The things we have seen tonight, Adam. Oh, the shame of
    this night!

England, again – and Christabel's former home, ample and
apparently serene in the summer sunshine.

Outside, on the terrace, Christabel, reading a novel, but
distractedly, is in a wicker chair in the bright sunshine. She lowers
her book to the sound of voices –
MR BURTON: (*Testily*) – well, that's rather the point, isn't it? That's
    precisely what Baldwin said. 'The bomber will always get
    through' –

Christabel's father and a local builder are emerging from what
looks like a half-submerged cavern on the far side of the tennis
court.

22

– And he's not wrong, is he? That's blindingly obvious!

BUILDER: (*Dubious*) That's as may be, Mr Burton. You'll still need a pump, though.

MR BURTON: What?

BUILDER: That there shelter's well below ground, sir –

MR BURTON: Of course it is!

Christabel watches her father and the builder as they move out of earshot.

BUILDER: Well, then. When it rains a bit, her'll fill up with water, sir, won't her – And wet's more like than war is, sir, if you don't mind my –

With a frown, she gets up, to cross the tennis court, to the air-raid shelter that her father is having built.

The shelter is gloomy, dank and unfinished. Christabel looks around it, pursing her lips. A moment. And then, with an ache –

CHRISTABEL: (*To herself*) Oh, Peter.

As she turns away, her father is there, peering at her.

MR BURTON: Better safe than sorry.

CHRISTABEL: Father, there isn't going to be a war.

MR BURTON: No?

CHRISTABEL: *No!*

They look at each other. Her exclamation is really about something else.

MR BURTON: Still. Better safe than sorry. Eh?

In Berlin, in a park, at the ornate bandstand, a smart military band plays a mix of martial and sentimental airs to lunchtime Berliners.

Beyond the slatted seats and the sandwich-eaters, two figures walk a path away from the bandstand.

ADAM: – and it's not isolated voices, by no means. But who, in the last resort – who can *really* act? The army.

PETER: The generals.

ADAM: The generals. *They* know we can't be catapulted into world war –

PETER: Can't be?

ADAM: Mustn't be!

Peter picks up a small stone, and throws it away.

PETER: 'Is' and 'Ought'.

ADAM: What?

PETER: The greatest chasm in the world.

Adam impatiently brushes this aside.

ADAM: The army is the only weapon capable of overthrowing this
   lot. The Wehrmacht! But when they arrest Hitler and his gang –

Peter seems depressed, withdrawn.

PETER: If. *If* they do.

Adam stops walking. The distant band oom–pahs.

ADAM: (*Angrily*) *When*, Peter. When that festering scum are
   rounded up and Adolf is kicking his heels in one of his own
   gaols –

A man, coming the other way, towards the band music, stares hard
at too-loud Adam.

PETER: Good afternoon.

He passes, staring, without acknowledgement.

ADAM: (*Mutter to* PETER) Sorry. Sorry.

But the man suddenly turns and calls back.

MAN IN PARK: Kicking his heels on the end of a *rope*, you mean!

He goes on towards the bandstand, with no backward glance.

PETER: (*Softly*) Well. Well.

Adam is immediately enthused again.

ADAM: And when it happens, Peter – rope or not – there has to be
   at least the nucleus of a *civilian* government capable of taking
   over. We have to have reliable support in every ministry,
   every department, every grade of the civil service –

PETER: Yes. Of course.

ADAM: (*Delighted*) Yes?

PETER: Yes. It makes sense, and – (*Sudden anguish.*) Oh, dear God.
   The chance. The idea. The very thought of actually being able
   to *do* something, to break this paralysis! I'd give anything to –
   (*Corrects himself.*) Anything. Except –

ADAM: I know.

PETER: My family.

ADAM: Peter. They are in the right place. You have done the right
   thing.

PETER: (*Wry*) Have I?

But Adam's face lights in sudden pleasure. Up ahead, clearly
waiting, is a young woman, Clarita.

24

ADAM: (*Calls*) Clarita!
Her face lights. She waves. Adam runs. Peter, standing off,
watches the eagerness of their embrace, with a pang.

Back in England, on the tennis court of her former home,
wop–p–p! Christabel serves an ace to her father, who was palpably
ready to receive it. She calls the score, with a glint of amusement.
CHRISTABEL: Forty–love.
MR BURTON: I say, Christabel. Be fair! Play the game, eh?
CHRISTABEL: What do you mean?
MR BURTON: You could hardly say I was ready. Now could you? I
    didn't even know the ball was in the air.
CHRISTABEL: Oh, Daddy!
MR BURTON: I mean, the damn ball was flying over the damn net
    before I'd begun to –
Christabel's mother, the two boys running ahead excitedly,
calling, 'Mummy!', has come out of the house, calling to her.
MRS BURTON: Christabel! Telephone! It's Germany calling – !
NICKY and JOHN: Mummy! Mummy! Quickly!
MR BURTON: But we are playing – ! It's a very close-run thing – !
Christabel has dropped her racket and jumped the net to get to the
house by the shortest possible route. Nicky has to call after her,
unable to keep up.
NICKY: (*In German*) Can I talk to Daddy? Mummy – ! Can I!
Mr Burton looks at his wife.
MR BURTON: Christabel really must teach these boys to speak
    properly. Living over there was one thing. But you don't have to
    dislocate your jaw trying to jabber in the way *they* do. Mmm?

Inside the house, eager, flushed, Christabel picks up the receiver –
CHRISTOBEL: (*On phone*) Hello? (*Then*) Hello? – Hello? Hello?

At the ministry building in Berlin, high up, close in, like a pigeon
on the sill, there is weathered grey stone showing the huge, silky,
shifting swastika banners between the tall windows – through
which Peter can be glimpsed in the indistinct embodiment of his
own reflection, speaking on the telephone.
PETER: Christabel! Christabel! Is that you – ? Is that – ? Hello –
    Hello? Hello?

Peter explodes in his office.

PETER: (*On phone*) Now listen, you! It's taken me all morning to get this connection – And now you're trying to tell me – *What?* Of course I have permission!

Back in England, Christabel still tries, on the other end of the broken connection.

CHRISTABEL: (*On phone*) Hello? Please – ? I cannot hear a – Hello? Nicky and John clutch demandingly at her tennis skirt, and her parents hover in the doorway. Upset, disappointed, Christabel gives up, and replaces the receiver.

CHRISTABEL: Nothing!

MR BURTON: But I thought Peter was supposed to be in their Foreign Office now – Don't they know how to use the telephone, or what?

MRS BURTON: (*Warning him*) Ssh, dear.

Christabel's eyes fill with tears.

In Berlin, irritated and frustrated, Peter is still trying to get a connection –

PETER: (*On phone*) Hello? Hello – ?

He looks up as an older man, Kreuze, enters without knocking. Instantly, Peter puts the phone down. Kreuze is a very senior official.

KREUZE: Perhaps we need to cultivate the skills of Joan of Arc. She, apparently, could listen to distant voices without unreliable outside apparatus.

Said amiably, it seems: yet somehow there is a chill.

PETER: Cheaper, too, sir.

Kreuze seems to stare. A feeling of tension.

KREUZE: Perhaps you should be in one of the economics departments.

PETER: Do they have telephones which work?

KREUZE: Oh – for *internal* calls – yes. I should think so. Settling in. Are you?

PETER: Thank you, sir. Yes.

Again, a disconcerting stare. Then – obscurely, politely menacing –

KREUZE: I thought you would like to know we have solved the little

26

problem of the anonymous letters within the ministry.

PETER: Oh. That is good news.

Kreuze smiles at him, tantalizingly.

KREUZE: The traitor gassed himself. He and his secretary. Last
night. The farewell note was full of invective and futile abuse.
There will be a few more arrests, no doubt. To smoke out any
others in his little circle. Mmm?

Smile fixed like an affectation. Kreuze nods and leaves, as softly as
he had arrived.

Peter stares at the closing door, tense, almost as though he
expects it to open again. It does. Kreuze's head comes around the
door –

I'm surprised you didn't ask who it was.

And he closes the door, properly.

Peter waits, nerves stretching. He picks up the telephone, puts it
down again. A moment. Then –

PETER: (*To himself*) Christabel.

Back in England –

CHRISTABEL: Stupid stupid phones! What *is* the point! I hear his
voice and then – nothing. What am I doing here?

MR BURTON: Being safe, that's what.

CHRISTABEL: My place is with Peter.

She says this evenly, without bravado or emphasis.

MRS BURTON: But, Christabel –

MR BURTON: Listen to your mother!

CHRISTABEL: (*Quietly*) I love you both dearly. I love this house. I
can breathe in this land. But – what is marriage for? What
were those vows all about? I have got to go back to Peter.

MR BURTON: (*Agitated*) You're not being sensible –

CHRISTABEL: (*Smile*) I'm afraid being sensible has nothing to do
with it.

The railway station, Berlin. Peter waits at the barrier, holding
flowers rather stiffly, but peering eagerly, as down platform a
locomotive expires in hisses of steam.

Behind him, as yet unseen by him, fully kitted and rifle-carrying
German troops are being marched into the station, preparing to be
transported eastward.

27

From the line of opening carriage doors, and the milling throng of arrivals, Christabel and the boys come into his view.

Her smile is swift, brilliant, as she sees him. The boys start to run.

The hugs, kisses and laughter which follow are gradually engulfed by the ranks of troops, and their words of joy and greeting lost in the hard, raucous shouts of the corporals.

Then, as the reunited Bielenbergs walk through the vast and crowded station –

CHRISTABEL: Oh – there are no flags. No drums. No trumpets.
      Yes, it's like an oasis, England – but *you* weren't there, Peter.
      And what's the use of that?

He looks sidelong at her, with an enigmatic smile.

      People say *If* this or *What If* that. It's all Perhaps and Might
      Be, this talk of war and stuff –

PETER: Perhaps. Might be.

CHRISTABEL: Exactly!

PETER: Christabel, my love, you don't seem to –

CHRISTABEL: (*Half-laugh*) I *hate* Politics. What has it to do with
      me? With us? With Nicky and John?

But 'she doth protest too much'. He looks sidelong again, as one unsure whether to speak of a particular thing or not. Then he does: almost brutally.

PETER: What has it to do with us? With the children? Well – you
      remember their doctor, you recall Professor Bauer?

CHRISTABEL: What do you mean, remember? (*Incredulous laugh*.)
      Peter. Of course I do! I've only been away a few –

PETER: (*Interrupting*) He's dead.

CHRISTABEL: *What* – ?

PETER: He hanged himself.

Christabel's intake of breath is painfully sharp and affecting. He looks at her swiftly, wondering if he has done the right thing.

      (*Gently*) Christabel?

She puts her hands to her face, deeply upset, for the moment unable to talk.

In the garden of the Bielenberg house, four-year-old Nicholas is pushing his younger brother, John, on a tricycle. John is laughing.

Christabel comes out, drying her hands on a bright pinafore.

CHRISTABEL: Nicky! John! Who wants their tea.

NICKY: What is it?

CHRISTABEL: I'm not telling you – (*Laugh.*) But I've made some
cakes!

They come running.

JOHN: Chocolate – ?

CHRISTABEL: Chocolate.

NICKY: Oo, good! Can Herr Neisse have one, Mummy?

JOHN: Can he?

CHRISTABEL: But he's not here – It's past his time . . .

NICKY: He's changing in the shed –

CHRISTABEL: (*Laugh*) What do you mean, changing in the shed?
What into? A butterfly –

She stops, suddenly. Neisse is coming out of the Toolshed in full
Nazi Brownshirt uniform.

Neisse, seeing her, calls across the lawn, apologetic.

NEISSE: Afternoon, Frau Bielenberg! Hope you don't mind – Only
there ent time for me to get home and change afore the
meeting – !

Christabel, shocked, manages an ambiguous flap of her hand.

CHRISTABEL: The kettle – !

She rushes back into the house.

NEISSE: (*Laugh; to the boys*) You see. A woman's work is never
done. That's why you must always be good boys to your mum.

In the kitchen, Christabel grips the edge of the sink, absorbing the
shock.

NICKY: Mummy. Herr Neisse's come for his cake.

JOHN: Chocolate!

Neisse, in brown garb, thumb hitched into his leather belt,
grinning like a simple man, is at the back door, holding the boys by
the hand.

NEISSE: Bet you be glad to be back, eh, Frau Bielenberg?

CHRISTABEL: I –

NEISSE: Come on, lads! Show Mum!

The two small boys shoot out their right arms, with piping voices.

NICKY and JOHN: (*Together*) *Heil Hitler!*

In Peter and Christabel's bedroom, late, a scritch–scratch of a match and its sudden flare as a cigarette is lit in the half-dark by Peter. He is sitting on his bed. The throaty Tick–h Tock–h from the big clock downstairs begins to obtrude.

Christabel turns as she wakes. She focuses. Sits up.

CHRISTABEL: (*Quietly*) Peter – ?

PETER: (*Whisper*) Sssh. My love.

CHRISTABEL: (*Whisper*) What's the matter . . .?

PETER: The clock. That damned clock.

CHRISTABEL: What?

PETER: Listen to it.

She listens. Tick–h Tock–h Tick–h Tock–h. But then –

CHRISTABEL: (*Frown*) Peter?

PETER: (*Wry*) Wouldn't it be nice if I could stop it?

CHRISTABEL: But you can.

He puts out his cigarette, scarcely smoked, and looks at her in the half-light.

PETER: Time. I mean, time.

CHRISTABEL: Ah. Well.

PETER: I want to stop it. Before it goes over the edge.

They look at each other. She puts out her long, bare arms to him.

CHRISTABEL: (*Softly*) Wait for one more hour. And *then* you can stop it.

He moves to her, swiftly, and they hold each other. Their passion grows, 'I'm Following You' fades in, very gradually, without words.

Memory drifts in as they make love.

Christabel is studying herself in the long mirror on the morning of her wedding day, deciding where to pin the lavender on her flowing white dress.

'I'm Following You' comes (in the band-only section) from the wind-up gramophone in the room.

The music continues uninterrupted as, in the hall of the Berlin house, the pendulum swings and glints and swings –

Upstairs, Peter and Christabel are in each other's arms.

The music slowly fades as Christabel's father, a lone figure as stiff as a scarecrow, stands in the middle of a sweep of his cropped lawn, looking up intently at the sky.

NEVILLE CHAMBERLAIN: *I am speaking to you from Number Ten Downing Street. This morning the British Ambassador in Berlin handed the –*

In Berlin, Nicky and John are whooping and laughing on the garden swing, oblivious.

The overlap of Chamberlain's voice upon itself is unsettling, alienating.

NEVILLE CHAMBERLAIN: *– the British Ambassador in Berlin handed the German Government a final note stating that unless –*

As was seen by Christabel from the car, but now day not night, as picture after picture of Adolf Hitler, with slogans and swastikas, move by.

The Chamberlain overlap still unsettling –

NEVILLE CHAMBERLAIN: *– German Government a final note stating that unless the British Government heard from them –*

The last overlap is on the 'unless', as the Chamberlain voice comes out of the radio in the Bielenberg living room.

Peter holds Christabel's hand as they sit together, listening. Adam, standing, leans on the mantel, blank in expression.

NEVILLE CHAMBERLAIN: (*On radio*) *– unless the British Government heard from them by eleven o'clock that they were prepared at once to withdraw their troops from Poland, a state of war would exist between us –*

Peter and Christabel are in each other's arms, in their bedroom, in the same sequence that had begun with the scritch–scratch of the striking match.

Outside, silence, in the moon-silvered darkness, except for the first creak-creak of the children's swing as it moves in the night breeze, rather eerily.

Then, suddenly, unexpectedly, and very close, a nightingale begins to sing, liquid and dramatic.

Christabel has come to the bedroom window, in her nightgown, to listen to the nightingale.

Peter comes up alongside her. A moment.

PETER: (*Quietly*) You see. There *is* a nightingale after all.

They listen – but now, somehow, they seem just a little apart.

CHRISTABEL: War.

PETER: Yes.

CHRISTABEL: Between our countries.

The nightingale stops singing, as suddenly as it had begun.

PETER: Yes. But – not us. Not between us. (*A moment.*) Christabel?

CHRISTABEL: No. Not us.

PETER: Christabel – ?

She does not look at him.

CHRISTABEL: If someone ever asks me about the night war was declared, I shall remember every detail. Every single thing. And most of all I shall remember the feeling of being –

She stops.

PETER: Yes?

She doesn't answer at once, nor look at him.

Christabel.

She turns, looks.

CHRISTABEL: Trapped. The feeling of being – (*Bleakly*) Trapped.

TWO

In a Berlin kindergarten, in December 1939, very young children pleasing teacher, chanting or singing in unison.

There is a big map of Germany on the wall – with new frontiers – and the standard portrait of Hitler.

INFANTS: O dear God
       I pray to Thee
       That I will ever be
       A good little child
       For Germany.
       Keep safe, O God,
       With thy strong hand
       Our beloved
       Fatherland.

And Nicky is amongst the children, reciting.

Groups of young mothers are gathering in the steadily falling snow outside the infant school.

A moment of smiling, chattering, mutual greeting.

RADIO VOICE: *Dear German mothers! Yuletide is at the door, and we must think of our little ones – but also of course of our purses . . .*

Christabel is arriving, hand in hand with John, to await Nicky. She smiles and chats with some of the other young mothers. They look up at the sky and complain of the weather.

– Above all, we must think, though, of our leader, who has dedicated his life to our future, and who calls on our –

The infants come rushing out of the school, exuberant, clutching picture postcards.

– our spirit of self-sacrifice. Let us think now, dear mothers, let us help you with your choice of Yuletide gift –

A small boy greets his mother, who kisses him warmly. He proudly shows her his postcard: it turns out to be a portrait of Hitler.

The mother, Ilse, instinctively reacts, her smile becoming almost a snarl. She grabs at the postcard as though to crumple it – and then quickly controls herself.

A quick glance around to see if anyone has noticed. Her eye falls on Christabel, who has. The two women hold glances. And there is a discreet nod or gleam of reassurance from Christabel.

> *– which will bring a sparkle into the lovely eyes of your family and at the same time save as many of those precious raw materials so needed by our leader for the fulfilment of his great task.*

Nicky, skipping, is one of the last to come out and show his mother his lantern and card.

CHRISTABEL: Nicky! Why are you always one of the last!

NICKY: Look. See!

He thrusts the postcard at her.

CHRISTABEL: Yes, dear.

NICKY: The Great – um – The Greatest Man Who Ever Lived.

CHRISTABEL: Oh. Well –

NICKY: Teacher said!

Christabel and Ilse have gravitated towards each other, and are walking away together, the children running a little ahead.

RADIO VOICE: *What about a Certificate of Aryan Ancestry – a splendid gift of lasting value? And for the little ones, a school satchel, for instance, made by Mother's loving hand out of –*

The radio voice ends abruptly on Ilse's contemptuous laugh.

ILSE: – Mother's loving hand, out of her old macintosh!

CHRISTABEL: Get soaked to the skin, Mother dear. It's all for the good of the cause.

ILSE: (*Stops laughing.*) Dear God. It's not just the stuff they put on the radio. What do they tell them in school?

CHRISTABEL: In my day when we put our hands up it was to ask if we could go to wee-wees.

Ilse sort of laughs, looks sideways.

ILSE: What did you say your husband does – ?

A sudden caution changes Christabel's face. And the tone of the conversation.

CHRISTABEL: I didn't. (*Then*) Oh, look at this snow, it always makes me think of fairy tales. Ogres and giants. And wicked witches.

Elsewhere in the city, the snow has whitened the looming grey ministry buildings enclosing the courtyard, where cars with chains on their wheels are parked. Two overcoated figures emerge from one of the official buildings, carrying briefcases.

PETER: (*Gloomily*) Adam. I feel that everything is static.

ADAM: (*Laugh*) Frozen. Do you mean?

PETER: Paralysis. Paralysis. Something that sits on your chest. I wake up with it.

ADAM: He's bound to move soon.

Peter knocks snow off the windscreen of his rackety little car.

PETER: Are you trying to cheer me up? Or are you determined to depress me?

ADAM: (*Shiver*) Christ! It's cold.

They sit hunched into themselves in the parked car, talking quietly, earnestly.

ADAM: Listen – the situation demands it. His own psychology demands it. All those overblown boasts! The unbendable will!

PETER: 'I will defeat France in open combat – '

ADAM: (*Chortle*) ' – in a matter of weeks.'

PETER: (*Smile*) 'And then turn my might against Russia.'

They laugh. They fall silent. Then –

ADAM: As soon as he launches all-out war, even the most hesitant will no longer be bound by the oath of allegiance – because the very existence of Germany will be called into question. (*At* PETER's *silence*) Peter?

PETER: (*Shiver*) Suppose. Just suppose –

He stops. Adam looks at him. They both feel another sort of chill.

ADAM: Go on.

Peter doesn't answer, but tries to start the car. Whirr–whirr–r–r–

Adam half snorts, opens the car door.

See you tomorrow.

Adam, about to shut the car door, almost angrily, instead leans in to (sort of) grin at Peter.

ADAM: *Suppose* pigs had wings. That's the only way they could get across the Maginot Line. Oink–oinking to the pork butchers.

He shuts the door, lifts his hand, and, bending into the snow-flurrying wind, goes to his own car.

35

Peter tries the ignition again. Whir–whirr–rr–
PETER: (*Clenched teeth*) But *suppose* . . .
And the car starts with a Bang! from the exhaust.

A cinema. On screen, a German newsreel shows victorious Panzer divisions smashing their way deep into France: scenes in a German film celebrating the fall of France.

Crowded audience, swathes of cigarette smoke in the projection beam, and eager faces, row upon row in the flickering light, as a blazing triumph is swaggeringly celebrated on the cinema screen.

Finding Christabel and Peter, expressionless, surrounded by joy.

Huge against the half-silhouettes of the audience, the screen images are now full of Nazi flags and banners: and then, a beaming Hitler.

COMMENTATOR: Germans! Unfurl the flags! Let church bells ring! Give highest honour to the Greatest Warlord of All Time!

Row upon row, the audience erupts in wild applause and cheers and whistles and foot-stamping.

Christabel and Peter, hardly daring to look at each other, are lost in a sea of enthusiasm. Martial music.

The cinema screen freezes the picture of Hitler. The music stops. The tumultuous applause dies away.

There is the briefest moment of the strangest silence, and then, to the roll of drums from the cinema's speakers – the German anthem, 'Deutschland über Alles'.

Tip–tip–tip go the seats, as the audience stands. The music swells, brassily heavy. The audience sings the anthem. With fervour and pride, as face upon face, row upon row now shows.

Peter and Christabel's sing, too, as they must. Catch at Christabel's covert sidelong glance at her German husband. Is he singing too loudly? Are his eyes shining? Shoulders straightening?

No? Not quite. Maybe not . . . but her own eyes moisten in a grief she cannot for the moment share with a living soul.

In the foyer of the cinema, as people flock out, a boisterous youth

entertains his friends and some others with a jeering and
inaccurate 'Marseillaise' for comic effect.
YOUTH: March–ons! March–ons!
      Dee–dee–Pom–Pom–
      Au Victoire – Da Da!
Others laugh at his floppy 'I surrender' postures, and his mates
hoot and jeer.

On a crowded train after they have left the cinema, Peter and
Christabel have the manner of a couple on edge.
PETER: (*Hesitant*) Do you want to go for a drink, or – ?
She shakes her head, subdued.
    Accordion music grows – and it sounds evocatively familiar. Is
this a dream?
CHRISTABEL: (*Gasp*) Oh!
A strange-looking man is playing a familiar little French tune on
his accordion, 'Sur le pont d'Avignon'.
    The dream becomes more troubled –

Big pools of silk on the lawn of Christabel's home in England
duplicate the fat, silvery moon: they are parachutes.
    The windows turn sudden, lustrous silver in moonlight, then –
CRASH!
    Springing out of their own crouching silhouettes against the
glittering panes, German stormtroopers rifle-butt their way in.

Christabel's father, snarling with fear and rage, tries to defend
himself with a golf club against the steel-helmeted soldiers as they
clatter up the stairs.
    From higher up, and weirdly, the sounds of 'I'm Following
You', on a distant gramophone, but in accordion music.
    Mr Burton falls back helplessly on the stairs. He screams as the
Nazi soldiers smash their rifle butts down on him.
    The screams die in a bloody gurgle as they repeatedly bayonet
him, to the distant, wistful strains of the song.

In her old room, Christabel turns from the long mirror in her
flowing white wedding dress.

The gramophone is playing 'I'm Following You'.

Her smile turning to terror as the door crashes in.

Standing there, at the head of the soldiers, is an officer in a black uniform, staring at her. He lifts his pistol to kill. It is *Peter*.

PETER: (*In reality*) *Christabel!*

In the bedroom in Berlin, Christabel rears up, sweating, out of a gasping nightmare, and Peter trying to wake or to reassure her –

PETER: Christabel – !

For a brief moment, half in and half out of nightmare, she starts to fight him off.

Then grief floods in at the moment of realization.

CHRISTABEL: (*Choke*) Peter? Oh – Peter . . .

PETER: It's all right – it's all right –

His arms are around her. She yields. And then almost at once straightens, to look at him, half accusingly.

CHRISTABEL: You. It was you.

PETER: (*Puzzled*) Darling – ?

CHRISTABEL: Peter. You were – Oh, Peter! What is going to happen?

PETER: (*Cautiously*) In the war – do you mean?

CHRISTABEL: In the war – yes – no – I mean, *us* – if our countries –

He takes hold of her, firmly.

PETER: This is not a war between *us* – Not you and me, Christabel! – And nothing can make it so. Nothing!

She looks at him. Then –

CHRISTABEL: (*Flat*) Germans. Unfurl the flags. Let church bells ring.

PETER: (*Deeply hurt*) Oh. My love.

She stays looking at him. Then her defencelessness suddenly shows.

CHRISTABEL: I –

PETER: (*Moved*) Chrislein. I cherish you.

A beat.

CHRISTABEL: Cherish.

PETER: What about it – ?

CHRISTABEL: Nice word.

PETER: What – ?

CHRISTABEL: Nice.
PETER: Christabel, I –
CHRISTABEL: (*Smile*) Sshh.
She puts a finger on his lips.
PETER: (*Moved*) Christabel.
CHRISTABEL: Sshh.
Her finger is still on his lips. He kisses it. Nibbles. They begin to caress, with an increasing passion.

In the daytime garden, Neisse is up a ladder, picking cherries or getting a cat out of a tree.
    Nearby, church bells are clanging, for German victory. A muffled radio voice begins to be heard . . .
WINSTON CHURCHILL: – *the Battle of France is over. I expect the Battle of Britain is about to begin. Upon this battle depends the survival of Christian civilization –*
Nicky and John are looking up the ladder, offering advice.

In the hall, children's toys are scattered about – wooden bricks, farm animals, London bus, an 'Alice' book in English.
WINSTON CHURCHILL: – *The whole fury and might of the enemy must very soon be turned on us. Hitler knows that he will have to break us in this island –*

Christabel alone in the living room, sits close to the set, ear almost against it, hand on the tuning knob, face intensely listening.
WINSTON CHURCHILL: – *or lose the war. Let us therefore brace ourselves to our duty and so bear ourselves that if the British Empire and its Commonwealth lasts for a thousand years men will still say, 'This was their finest –*
Click! Christabel chops off a legendary sentence, for –
    Half a dozen formidable ladies form a phalanx in the doorway. They are in long grey macintoshes and huge steel helmets, and their arms are shooting out in stiff unison.
THE LADIES: Heil Hitler!
CHRISTABEL: (*Flustered*) What – ?
They wait, Nazi to the corset bone. Christabel gives a sort of half-hearted flap rather than the authentic salute.
    Heil.

39

They stare, eyes like hard-boiled sweets.

FIRST LADY: We are your branch of the Air Defence League.

SECOND LADY: Your gardener said to come in –

FIRST LADY: Why were you listening to the wireless in that manner?

Christabel feels all the hard eyes upon her.

CHRISTABEL: What did you say?

She cups her hand to her ear, her composure returning.

FIRST LADY: You *do* know it is a criminal offence to listen to foreign broadcasts?

THIRD LADY: A law to protect us.

SECOND LADY: From Moral Self-Mutilation.

Christabel rises, in her best English-patrician manner.

CHRISTABEL: I cannot quite catch all that you say. But if I am correct in detecting a personal remark, kindly take yourselves off!

A flutter of disconcerted expressions under the helmets.

FIRST LADY: Are you saying you are hard of hearing?

CHRISTABEL: (*Classically*) What?

The first lady frowns at her clipboard.

FIRST LADY: (*Very loudly*) Frau Bielenberg. It says you are English born –

CHRISTABEL: (*Very loudly*) Correct!

The ladies' expressions mirror-image an English assumption that foreigners are odd, probably stupid, and made to understand only by speaking *at* them very slowly and very loudly.

FIRST LADY: (*Very loud*) You are required to protect yourself from British terrorist air raids. Your cellar must be reinforced, with an emergency exit. Do–you–understand – ?

CHRISTABEL: (*Very loud*) No. I don't!

A flutter of scorn, or pitying amusement, under the helmets.

FIRST LADY: It–is–very–simple–you –

CHRISTABEL: (*Cutting in*) Perhaps I haven't heard properly again. But – (*Puzzled innocence*) – didn't Reichsmarschal Goering say that he would take a Jewish name if just *one* British bomber got through to our beloved Berlin?

Silence. They stare. She smiles back, sweetly. Then –

FIRST LADY: Comply with the Law!

CHRISTABEL: What?

They look at her, bewildered. The first lady shoots out her arm.
FIRST LADY: Heil Hitler!
And this time they do not wait for an answering salute. Christabel
watches them go, then puts her hand to her face to repress her
triumphant hilarity.

A conference room at the ministry, which is, except for the
dominating portrait of Hitler, an elegant room, with a long
polished table. Gathered in one corner, in a haze of cigarette
smoke and murmuring male conversation, are about a dozen
committee members.
    Kreuze is taking his place at the head of the table, and begins to
tap down and square off his papers. The members, showing
regard for each other's precedence, stand at their chairs.
    Kreuze looks up with the pretence of one just a little irritated
by formality, and nods briskly.
    They all sit, and do as he did, tapping down and squaring off
their papers. Then silence.
KREUZE: Good afternoon, gentlemen.
MEMBERS: (*Murmur*) Good afternoon.
Silence. Kreuze seems always on the brink of some secret or
mysterious amusement.
KREUZE: Heil Hitler.
MEMBERS: (*Brisker*) Heil Hitler!
Kreuze presses a button. A door opens. Into the room comes a
strikingly attractive young woman, Lexi, who sends out an air of
sophisticated disdain. The members try not to be affected by her
sexuality, but not all succeed.
    Lexi sits to the side and a little to the rear of Kreuze, takes out
pen and papers, crosses her long legs, waits: with little of a
secretarial manner.
KREUZE: Good. Good. The England Committee is now in session.
    And there is only one item on the agenda. Lexi.
LEXI: (*Mannered drawl*) One colon the military defeat and
    occupation of England and stroke or prior request for peace
    stop brackets to be understood and hereinafter referred to as
    British Surrender stop brackets.

Christabel's former house in England is seen from the air. The picture tilts as the aircraft from which it is seen banks and dives, engines roaring.

Christabel's father, dozing under *The Times*, opens one fierce eye and fixes it on the heavens.

A comically incredulous moment as he realizes that it is a German plane, coming in very, very low: a JU–22 reconnaissance plane.

He stands, astounded, indignant, peering into the sky – then, enraged, runs into the house.

The young German pilot (later identified) peers down at the loomingly closer and closer view of Christabel's family home.

Christabel's enraged father runs to the middle of the lawn, bearing a double-barrel shotgun. He swings it into aim, comically but bravely ineffective, and blasts off both barrels, heavenwards.

Back in Berlin, an official Mercedes, sporting swastika, sweeps through saluting guards into an inner courtyard of the ministry.

As the military driver opens the door for his passengers – Kreuze, Peter, Adam and another FO official, Botho.

KREUZE: – ideally, therefore, a negotiated peace that is *ipso facto* a surrender – I'm not concerned with pendantries.

As they get out of the car –

Common sense says there's no need to pulverize the English into ashes. Attractive though *that* thought is to people of *my* generation.

BOTHO: But won't the Empire be –

KREUZE: (*Contemptuously*) Oh. I think we're quite capable of whipping a few niggers into order, don't you?

He looks at them, provocatively, then turns away like someone in a hurry to talk to more important listeners.

Peter, Adam and Botho stand together, watching Kreuze disappear into the grey hulk of buildings.

BOTHO: Sometimes it helps if you stick two fingers down your throat.

PETER: That's about all we can do, Botho. Vomit!

BOTHO: (*Gloomily*) If England sues for peace –
ADAM: Then we're all done for! Finished! Everything –
everywhere – for as far ahead as anyone can see.
They look at each other, and each seems to acknowledge the truth
of what has just been said. Then –
PETER: (*Quietly*) They'll fight.
BOTHO: Even after they're invaded? Will they let London be
razed to the ground?
PETER: I'm sure of it. (*Faint smile.*) They are a pig-headed lot,
believe me. I'm an expert!
Adam is looking at Peter intently. He nods.
ADAM: We have go to get on to the England Committee.
PETER: And do what?
ADAM: *If* the British keep fighting, and are occupied – then
there'll be a genuine Resistance. A structure.
BOTHO: And plenty of collaborators – you can be sure of that.
Blue-bloods who hate Jews. Big businessmen who care only
for order on the factory floor.
PETER: Then we need to know them! The England Committee is
bound to have a list already.
ADAM: Exactly. But the others – it cannot only be the party or the
Gestapo they will encounter. They'll need us. We'll need
them.

At the railway station, what looks at first to be a normal squad of
marching British soldiers, singing – swiftly revealed to be
prisoners-of-war, guarded by armed German soldiers.
BRITISH SOLDIERS: (*Sing*) We had ter join
We had ter join
We had ter join the soddin' army
Five bob a week
Sod all to eat
Great big boots
And blisters on yer feet –
As they march into the railway yard, the guards bellow for
silence.

A train slowing, clank–clank, to enter the station, full to the
corridors, crowded with servicemen, and some civilians.

The pilot of the German plane seen earlier, Albrecht, is with his mother, Peter's Aunt Ulla. Stooping, he looks out, and smiles –

ALBRECHT: We must tell Christabel.

AUNT ULLA: Oh – but won't it upset her?

A line of khaki figures passing bricks from one to the other, under the eyes of their guards.

In the Bielenberg living room a blown-up Luftwaffe aerial photograph of Christabel's English home is rolled open on a table by Albrecht with an impresario flourish.

CHRISTABEL: (*Gasp*) Albrecht! Oh, but this is – Oh, how *clever* of you!

She is overwhelmed. He is looking at her with a glint of amusement.

ALBRECHT: That was how it used to look, Christabel. *Before* I dropped –

AUNT ULLA: (*Sharply*) Albrecht!

PETER: (*Laugh*) It's all right, Chris. My cousin has always specialized in gallows humour.

ALBRECHT: Which is why I fly, of course.

CHRISTABEL: But you did this for *me* – ? I think it's – wonderful – !

She embraces him, warmly.

PETER: My God. You always *did* make me jealous. Aunt Ulla – why is he such a knight in shining armour?

ALBRECHT: It comes naturally.

AUNT ULLA: Oh, he enjoys showing off. Especially in front of lovely ladies.

ALBRECHT: *English* ladies. Lovely *English* ones.

He rolls his eyes at Christabel, mock lascivious. They laugh.

PETER: Aunt Ulla – please leave him at home next time.

CHRISTABEL: Oh no, you don't!

As Albrecht essays a courtly bow, Peter suddenly changes the mood.

PETER: Albrecht. Is Goering correct? Is it true the British have next to no air cover?

Albrecht straightens, his bow, his face, his manner. He looks at Peter, steady-eyed.

ALBRECHT: They have air cover. They will fight. It is going to be more difficult than people say.

At the railway station, the British prisoners, working in desultory fashion, have started to nudge and wink as they become aware of a woman paying close interest in them.

It is Christabel, at a wall above them.

CHRISTABEL: (*Calls*) We're not beat! We're not beaten yet!

And she throws a packet of cigarettes –

The effect is an instantaneous alertness, and her transformation from German bitch or whore to angel.

BRITISH SOLDIER: (*Calls*) We know that, darling! Don't you worry about it!

One after the other, rapid-fire, cigarette packets descend: but not all can be picked up before the chatting guards turn.

The guards, rifles slung, bored, pass along the line of prisoners, in which some have boots over the packets, some pretend to work, and all ignore Christabel.

Then a sudden, comic, efficient scrabble of retrieval as the guards turn again.

SOLDIER: (*Calls*) Godblessyaluv!

CHRISTABEL: And you – all of you!

One of the guards at last whips around, cocking his rifle.

GUARD: Work! Work!

Christabel hurries back to where Peter's ramshackle car is parked.

Peter, the boys, Albrecht and Aunt Ulla are waiting, discreetly separate from 'her' moment.

Peter looks at her closely. Her eyes glisten with emotion, but she is smiling with pleasure.

Albrecht and Aunt Ulla are being seen off by the Bielenbergs, at an about-to-depart train full of servicemen.

The railway guard shouts for the carriage doors to be closed.

CHRISTABEL: Nicky – John – Say goodbye to Aunt Ulla and Uncle Albrecht –

NICKY and JOHN: Bye Bye, Aunt Ulla – Uncle Albrecht!

CHRISTABEL: (*Severely*) And thank you for the presents.

NICKY and JOHN: And thank you for the presents!

So many hugs and kisses, at every window, all along the platform.

RAILWAY GUARD: (*Shouting*) Close the doors! Close the doors!

PETER: Albrecht. Be careful!

ALBRECHT: Bet your life!

AUNT ULLA: Christabel – I know what you must be feeling, my dear. God bless!

They are embracing, as whistles, shouts, and the whoompf! of steam signal departure, and the crowded train jerks into life.

ALBRECHT: Christabel! Come with me!

CHRISTABEL: Of course I will!

Albrecht is, like many others, leaning out of the window, waving farewell, in his smart Luftwaffe uniform.

All the length of the platform, families are saying goodbye to sons and husbands.

The Bielenbergs, feeling perhaps some sadness, like a premonition, are returning to their elderly car. It is a balmy August night (1940), but there are no lights.

PETER: Don't worry. Pilots have charmed lives. Well – pilots like Albrecht, anyway. The thorns wouldn't get him if he fell into a rose bush.

CHRISTABEL: (*Laugh*) But I think he already has!

But suddenly, like banshees, air-raid sirens are howling.

NICKY: Mummy – ?

CHRISTABEL: (*Reassuring*) Isn't it a *terrific* noise?

Someone is blowing a whistle. People are running past.

PETER: I suppose it had to come one day. Chris – it's look for a shelter, or go home.

She has instinctively taken hold of the children, but they are excited, not afraid.

CHRISTABEL: I'd rather we weren't in the middle of Berlin –

PETER: They'll be aiming for the station, that's for sure –

The siren howl almost deafens them.

CHRISTABEL: (*To the boys*) They won't hurt us.

NICKY: (*Excited*) It's Mummy's people! Isn't it? Isn't it?

PETER: Let's get out of here!

The car is crawling at near walking pace, its occupants more or less shadows.

But through the windscreen, the sky criss-crosses with sliding searchlight beams, and the anti-aircraft batteries have opened up.

CHRISTABEL: They must be directly overhead –

PETER: (*Calmly*) I think we have made a mistake.

Up ahead, an almighty explosion, and some buildings are collapsing across the street.

The car coming to an abrupt halt as the way ahead obscures further with belching smoke and debris.

NICKY: (*Shout of fear*) Daddy! Why are they doing it!

JOHN: Mummy!

CHRISTABEL: It's all right – all right –

PETER: Let's get out of this box. Come on! There's good lads –
    Take care of Mummy, eh? Help Mummy –

WHUMPF! of another bomb, much closer –

As the family hustles out of the car, crouching, scurrying, holding each other, the windows on one side of the car shatter into cascades of flying glass.

They reach inadequate (but nearest) cover – a doorway or low wall – just as blast waves whip, suck and howl along the street, like a sudden tornado, scattering debris and litter.

They crouch close, expecting another explosion –

JOHN: Mumm–eee – !

WHUMPH! very near, and an unearthly orange light, momentarily illuminating them as they clasp each other in a tight huddle.

Smoke clearing, and, although ack-ack guns are distantly firing and searchlights sweep, it is becoming clear that the raid is passing.

PETER: They're moving off – it's coming to an end. We're all
    right – ! (*Standing, he is gripped by sudden rage.*) Damn them!
    God damn the –

He stops, abruptly, and looks at Christabel.

NICKY: Have they gone? Have they?

PETER: (*Changed tone*) Yes. We're safe now. But I'm not so sure
    about the poor old car –

But he is still looking at Christabel, so taken by her expression.

She is looking up at the searchlit sky, and there is a strange and compelling glint in her eyes.

CHRISTABEL: (*Softly*) Safe home.

Then she realizes the words are not the most appropriate for those who nearly killed her family. She looks at Peter – who deliberately chooses to misunderstand.

PETER: Oh. We shall have to walk a long way. But we'll get home safe all right.

CHRISTABEL: (*Adjusting*) Of course we will!

She hugs the two boys, almost too much so.

NICKY: That means we can stay up *late*? Doesn't it? Doesn't it!

JOHN: Can we! Can we!

Peter lifts John up on to his shoulders, with a laugh.

PETER: You can, my lad! Late and – up on high.

They walk off, very much together.

At the ministry, beyond the array of Nazi flags, the high windows are now criss-crossed with anti-fragmentation tape.

WINSTON CHURCHILL: – *We will never parley, we will never negotiate with Hitler or any of his gang* –

Through the first window, a gaggle of officials and senior military officers are toasting the 'good news'.

A little way along – another window –

Languidly beautiful Lexi, with 1940s earphones, typing –

WINSTON CHURCHILL: – *We shall fight him by land, we shall fight him by sea, we shall fight him in the air* –

The Churchill words clack–clack–clacking on to the page.

– *until with God's help we have rid the earth of his shadow and liberated* –

In the park Christabel, Nicholas and John are feeding the ducks.

WINSTON CHURCHILL: – *its peoples from his yoke* –

A young soldier watches, from a discreet distance.

– *Any man or state who fights on against Nazidom will have our aid* –

The soldier is examining the little group wistfully: a yearning that seems to go beyond the obvious sexual one for a beautiful woman stooping attractively beside the pond.

48

At the ministry, meanwhile, headphoned Lexi is typing the same words –

WINSTON CHURCHILL: *Any man or state who marches with Hitler is our foe. That is our policy and that is our declaration.*

At the pond in the park Christabel becomes aware of the young German soldier, and registers the wistful intensity of his stare.

WINSTON CHURCHILL: *It follows therefore that we shall give whatever help we can to Russia and the Russian people. Let us redouble our exertions –*

The soldier, shy, looks away, then looks back again. Hesitantly, he manoeuvres himself closer.

In the ministry conference room, at the head of the long table, Kreuze takes up the Churchill voice, reading from the typescript –

KREUZE: (*Reading*) ' – and that is our declaration. It follows therefore that we shall give whatever help we can to Russia and the Russian people. Let us redouble our exertions and – ' What is this word? The letters are arse about tit.

Lexi, sitting at his side, leans in.

LEXI: Strike.

KREUZE: (*Sniff*) '*Strike* with united strength while life and blah–blah–blah–'

He discards the typescript, and looks around the table, at which sit a dozen men, now including Peter, Adam, and Botho.

Thus Churchill last night to the British people. Thus the braying of an ass. The man speaks as though he is full of pudding and pig-fat. But what *we* have to consider are not these – how shall we say? – these – farts of rhetoric – eructations of ignorance – but the implications upon English opinion of the German onslaught upon the Bolsheviks. (*Looks around.*) Well? Anyone?

Botho looks at Adam, sardonic. Then –

BOTHO: The English plutocrats will feel uneasy. They would rather attack the Soviet Union themselves.

KREUZE: Correct.

A MEMBER: They will not wish to see the Soviets survive –

KREUZE: (*Cuttingly*) Obviously.

ANOTHER MEMBER: Intensification of the English class war.

Kreuze stands, with a nasty smile.

KREUZE: The *real* implication of our invasion of Russia, gentlemen, is that England takes second place now. And *therefore* so does this committee. Professionally speaking, gentlemen, you are seriously *downgraded*.

Greatly amused, he glides away, leaving them to look at each other, sheepishly. Then –

ADAM: (*To* PETER) What is that Tipperary song – ? 'Goodbye, Tipperary.'

PETER: (*Laugh*) 'Farewell, Leicester Square.'

Some laughter. But most do not share it, and it dies, awkwardly.

OLDER MEMBER: (*Vigorously*) On to Final Victory!

Murmurs of assent, from all. Adam and Peter exchange swift glances.

In the park, Christabel and the boys listening to the young soldier.

YOUNG SOLDIER: (*Recites*) We travelled in the print of olden wars
    Yet all the land was green,
    And love we found, and peace,
    Where fire and war had been.
    They pass and smile, the children of the sword –
    No more the sword they wield;
    And O, how deep the corn
    Along the beautiful battlefield!

As soon as he stops, his posture becomes instantly awkward again – making Christabel feel a little awkward herself.

CHRISTABEL: Oh, that's – that's very nice.

YOUNG SOLDIER: I shall always remember this, gnädige Frau. Always. You. (*Awkwardly*) And the ducks.

They look at each other. Then Christabel extends her hand.

CHRISTABEL: Well – I wish you good luck. (*Laugh.*) And so do the ducks.

He hesitates, not wanting to go, then shakes her hand with a murmur.

JOHN: Where are you going?

YOUNG SOLDIER: I'm not allowed to say. Actually – I don't really

know. East. They say East. (*Shrug.*) Russia. The Bolshevik
Menace.
NICKY: Will you kill lots and lots?
JOHN: Stick them with your bayonet!
CHRISTABEL: Nicky. John. Say goodbye, now –
YOUNG SOLDIER: I shall fight for the Fatherland. There is no
    option. Do we have any choice?
He swallows, nods, then – in what he takes to be a soldierly
farewell –
    Heil Hitler!
She just stares, and his expression wavers. He drops his arm.
    (*Quietly*) Yes. Peace is better. I believe that with all my heart.
    Thank you.
Touched by his vulnerability, she suddenly, instinctively, kisses
him.
CHRISTABEL: Look after yourself.
Overwhelmed he gapes at her, comically, then with a strange
WHOOP! he turns and runs. She watches him go, smiling. He
turns, grins proudly, waves.
NICKY: (*Solemn*) I shall tell Dad.

The Bielenbergs are giving a party at their home. Beautiful Lexi
is receiving champagne, in her seemingly mannered drawl.
LEXI: Thank you, darling. I can accept acorn coffee and axel-
    grease butter. But life without *real* champagne would be too,
    too intolerable.
Christabel laughs, passing on, attending to a house full of guests.
CHRISTABEL: This is the last of our stocks, I promise. After that –
    methylated spirits!
Ilse, further along, has a cake in one hand, glass in the other.
ILSE: (*Calls*) Black marketeer!
CHRISTABEL: You bet!

The party spreads out into the hall. Peter is here, at the bottom of
the stairs, talking to Carl Langbehn.
PETER: (*Smile*) Sip it slowly, Dr Langbehn – there's not much of
    it left.
LANGBEHN: I think we must get used to things that diminish and
    then disappear – don't you?

51

They look at each other. Peter stops smiling.

PETER: Yes.

LANGBEHN: I presume that is why you stopped being a lawyer?

PETER: Sorry?

LANGBEHN: No Law.

Peter looks at him, carefully.

PETER: Ah. But you still practise, Dr Langbehn. Though not in court, I believe.

LANGBEHN: (*Shrug*) I pull the shreds and tatters around myself. I dodge and weave and argue and appeal – But when your country has fallen into the hands of criminals and gangsters – well, it is like shouting through the bars of a prison cell. Is it not?

Peter examines him. Noise and laughter all around.

PETER: Should you be saying this, Dr Langbehn?

Langbehn returns the look, the tone.

LANGBEHN: Should I not?

PETER: Carl – do you mind if I call you Carl – ?

LANGBEHN: Please do, Peter.

PETER: Forgive me, but – I know your work as a lawyer – I know you slightly as a neighbour – and I would not have asked you tonight if –

LANGBEHN: If I had been a Nazi.

Peter *must* be cautious.

PETER: Well, it's not so much that we – a question of congeniality, really. Politics is not my –

LANGBEHN: It's all right. I would not have come if I had not thought we were of the same opinion.

PETER: Which is?

LANGBEHN: I know that Hitler has to be removed. The question is no longer When. It is How.

They hold glances. Then Peter nods. They chink their glasses, not smiling, eyes hard.

Later, and an air of mild inebriation. Adam has his arm around Clarita.

ADAM: Attention! Attention! (*Imitates radio fanfare*) Ta, tara ta, tara ta, tara taa! Eine Sondermeldung!

CLARITA: (*Laugh*) Oh, stop it –

The babble of conversation dies.

ADAM: Clarita and I are very grateful to Christabel and Peter for celebrating our first wedding anniversary in this splendid pre-war fashion –

CHRISTABEL: We'd forgotten it *was* your anniversary, Adam.

Laughter.

CLARITA: So had I! On all fronts!

Renewed laughter.

Nicky and John peer down through the banisters at the sights and sounds of an adult party, reacting to the sound of adult laughter with indignant looks at each other.

ADAM: – So I want two volunteers for a *very* dangerous assignment.

Elaborate groans.

Two, please, to stand outside and keep watch – We are going to tune into – (*Mock horror.*)

The BBC in London. I happen to know that Christabel's favourite dance band is playing this very night! Don't dare ask *how* I know – four hundred good men lost their lives to crack the code!

Some laughter and applause: but also some unease. Christabel's eyes are bright with pleasure.

LEXI: Then what are we waiting for? Let's all swing together.

Two dark figures meet from opposite directions in the unlit road outside the house.

One cups his hands so that both can light cigarettes. The quick match-flare shows it to be Adam and Botho.

In the house, with occasional whee! and whistle the radio bounces out the BBC dance music.

The furniture is pushed back, and couples dance, including Peter and Christabel. And he steps on her toe.

Langbehn watches from the doorway, then turns away.

In the road outside, two figures in the dark, talking very quietly.

BOTHO: It's like having a rat trapped in a spiral inside your own head – Do *you* ever lose that feeling?

ADAM: What do you think?

BOTHO: I *can't* think. My head is in permanent chaos. And I wake up sweating. (*Laugh.*) That's when I don't wake up shivering, of course.

ADAM: (*Soft laugh*) Welcome to the club, Botho. Membership fees can be paid in an aspirin.

They look up and down the dark street. They fall silent. Then –

BOTHO: Are they all safe? Is everyone there to be trusted?

Adam grinds out his cigarette.

ADAM: (*Mordant*) Well. You'll know in – about a week.

In the house, cheek-to-cheek dancing, sleepily. And in strides – Adolf Hitler!

'ADOLF HITLER': (*Scream*) Traitors! Enemies of the Reich! Listening to Jew music!

A half-second of startled incredulity: the eye-popping figure, is, in this light, a frighteningly good imitation of the Führer.

And then a sudden release of huge laughter.

(*Scream*) You laugh? You laugh? You mock your leader! The greatest warlord of all time! The Genghis Khan of our day and age!

The laughter grows so much that it must have a tinge of hysteria.

'Hitler' cannot keep it up. His grin more easily reveals him as Langbehn.

Suddenly, Adam is running down a long, high and wide corridor at the ministry, like one possessed.

He collides with a clerk emerging from a door with an armful of files, but, though he scatters them, barely stops.

The little, bespectacled clerk, his files on the marbled floor, looks at the receding, running Adam.

CLERK: You heap of shit.

Adam, breathless, bursts into Peter's office, too excited for proper caution.

ADAM: (*Gasp*) Have you – have you got it – the news! Peter! We have declared war on America – ! You know what that *means*!

54

PETER: On to final victory!

ADAM: Wha–?

But he follows the slight tilt of Peter's head, and –
> Final Victory!

A black-uniformed SS colonel is coming through from the outer office.
> Adam, brimming over, has started to laugh, in a helpless excess –

SS COLONEL: What is it? Why do you laugh?

ADAM: (*Made worse*) I – I've always – Hoo! Hoo! – Sorry. But I've always wanted to – Hoo! Hoo! Hooo!

SS COLONEL: (*Frown*) What's the matter with you?

Peter looks at Adam in despairing admonition as Adam tries to control his face – and attempts rescue.

PETER: Herr von Trott was saying only yesterday, Colonel, that he always wanted to – to – put his boot in the face of Mickey Mouse. We are speaking metaphorically, Colonel. A – a – reference to American culture.

ADAM: Exactly! And that duck. Speaking metaphorically.

SS COLONEL: (*Blank*) What duck?

Adam and Peter look at each other – then both burst into uninhibited laughter. The colonel stares at them, genuinely puzzled, very irritated.

PETER: I'm – (*Gurgle*) – I'm s-s–

The unamused colonel decides to leave, shooting out his arm as a sort of punishment.

SS COLONEL: Heil Hitler!

Adam and Peter make huge efforts at self-control.

ADAM and PETER: Heil Hitler!

The colonel leaves, in a small huff. As Adam and Peter catch glances again, they cannot help resuming their barely suppressed laughter. Adam imitates Donald Duck, almost perfectly.

ADAM: Quack–quack–quaaaaack – !

They stop laughing, as though a switch has been turned off. They look at each other, searchingly, solemnly. And then quietly, swiftly embrace.

At the Bielenberg house Christabel, looking upset, opens the front door on Ilse, and a middle-aged, very blonde woman with lowered eyes.

ILSE: (*Worried*) Christabel – I *know* this isn't the time – I mean, I know how upset you must be about – about –

CHRISTABEL: (*Dully*) Albrecht. Yes. Shot down.

ILSE: I suppose there's no chance he –

CHRISTABEL: No. He didn't bail out. He was killed. The news is definite.

ILSE: I'm so sorry.

CHRISTABEL: He was a fine – (*Shivers.*) I liked him. I liked him a lot, and now – (*She seems to see the stranger for the first time.*) But please. Come on in. I'm sorry. I'm not myself. I – Come in.

Ilse's companion does not lift her eyes.

In the living room –

ILSE: I didn't know where else to try next. Christabel. As you can see, Freda has dyed her hair. She can easily pass for Aryan.

Christabel looks at Freda, who looks away.

CHRISTABEL: Ilse –

ILSE: (*Quickly*) The house she's been hiding in with her husband – it's being watched. Jacob dare not go out in the day, else he'd – He looks too Jewish, Christabel.

Christabel again looks at Freda, who again looks away.

They've taken off their Stars of David, you see.

CHRISTABEL: (*To Freda*) Does that mean you don't get a ration card?

Like a child unwilling to answer, Freda looks at Ilse.

ILSE: They have no identity, officially. They've gone under.

FREDA: (*Suddenly*) Below the waves.

Slightly surprised, now, by the interjection, they look at her. But she again lowers her eyes, nervously twisting and turning her wedding ring.

ILSE: Freda is willing to take on any housework – and her husband could live in your cellar, if –

CHRISTABEL: Peter's not here, and – This is not something I feel I –

ILSE: A little while, that's all. They want to get out of Berlin – and – Christabel. I know the risk. I know what is being asked.

CHRISTABEL: The children.

ILSE: Yes. The children.

They look at each other. Christabel has to move about, agitated.
She goes to the window. She looks at Ilse. She looks out. Then –

CHRISTABEL: If we were caught – Nicky and John would be
	virtual orphans. It would destroy *their* lives as well as our
	own.

ILSE: (*Quickly*) The same is true in my house.

Christabel hesitates.

CHRISTABEL: There's something else. I – But I can't tell you.

ILSE: Peter?

CHRISTABEL: His work. In the –

She stops, unwilling to say more.

ILSE: Can you – *ask* him – ? Would you put it to him?

CHRISTABEL: He's gone to see his Aunt – Albrecht's mother.
	She's – He won't be back until tomorrow. I don't think I –
	Oh God! Illse. Please. I –

Christabel has avoided looking at Freda in the last few speeches,
but now she does, helplessly.
	Freda raises her eyes, and looks full at Christabel, her
expression closer to challenge or accusation than to supplication.

At night, outside, just discernible, the figure of a lurking man
staring at the dark house, like one keeping discreet surveillance.

In the children's bedroom, Christabel reads the boys an English
story.

CHRISTABEL: (*Reads*) 'The cause of lightning,' Alice said very
	decidedly, for she felt quite sure about this, 'is the thunder –
	no, no!' she hastily corrected herself. 'I meant the other way.'

NICKY: Mum?

CHRISTABEL: (*Reading*) 'It's too late to correct it,' said the Red
	Queen: 'when you've once said a thing – '

Her voice trails off into self-absorbed anxiety.

NICKY: (*Puzzled*) Mum?

John has fallen asleep.

CHRISTABEL: Sorry. (*Smiles.*) 'When you've once said a thing,
	that fixes it, and you must take the consequences.'

Outside the lurker waits. A police siren ooh–ahs in the distance.
He seems to cower even deeper into the shadows.

At the house opposite, the curtains of an upstairs room twitch open. It is Langbehn, looking out. He stops dead. He can see the dark shape of a lurking man watching the Bielenberg house. He peers and peers, then hisses under his breath.

In the hall of the Bielenberg house, the pendulum swings and glints on the throatily ticking clock. And a tense Freda watches it. Five to nine.

The telephone jangles, and Freda jumps, then stares at the ringing phone, in fear.

Christabel comes running down the stairs to answer it.

In the upstairs study of the house opposite, Langbehn uses the phone like one who knows it is tapped.

LANGBEHN: (*On phone*) Ah. Christabel. Langbehn here. Been turning out an old cupboard. I was – ah – I wonder if your lads would like my old copy of the story I've just come across. The Three Little Pigs and the Wolf – ?

Christabel on her phone in the hall.

CHRISTABEL: (*Puzzled*) Oh, I think they're getting just a little past that now, Carl – but . . .

LANGBEHN: (*On his phone*) Now, now. One's never too old for stories with a lesson in them – (*Laugh*.) If I *concentrate* – I was so fond of that tale! – If I *concentrate*, Christabel, I can see the wolf now, standing outside the house! (*Laugh*.) I always wanted to tell the piggies, but of course there was no way of doing that!

He waits, tense.

Freda is still watching the clock in the hall of the Bielenberg house. Christabel stiffens.

CHRISTABEL: (*On phone*) Well, yes. (*Forced laugh*.) Now that you remind me of it, I think the boys might very well like to see the book, Carl. The wolf outside – yes. Yes. (*Laugh*.) They're more or less asleep now. But I will go and see. (*Masks the phone, speaks to Freda*.) There is someone outside.

Freda, face contorting with nerves, points at the clock, and whispers.

FREDA: Jacob. Nine o'clock. Jacob!
Christabel frowns, nods, resumes the phone conversation.
CHRISTABEL: But sometimes, you know, the poor old wolf is
   unfairly treated in fairy tales, Carl. Perhaps the poor thing
   only wanted shelter.

Freda comes out of the house, cautious, looking around and
about, in the dark.
   The lurker has moved to the shrubs, closer to the house.
THE LURKER: (*Whisper*) Freda?
He comes clear of the bushes. They look at each other, in dark
silence. Then Freda takes his hand, and leads him towards the
house.

In his study, Langbehn flicks aside the curtain again, to look out.
   He sees the two figures go into the darkened house, and he
frowns.

In the daytime garden, Nicky and John happily at play, laughing
on the swing.
JOHN: (*Sings*) See-saw! Margery Daw!
NICKY: No! No! That's an *English* song!
The swing creaks as it moves.

Freda taking food and drink on a tray to Jacob, who has a candle
alight, and blankets around himself, in the cellar of the
Bielenberg house.
JACOB: Freda. I can hear children. There are children in this
   house.
FREDA: Yes.
Looking sad-eyed at her, he slowly shakes his head.

In the living room above, Langbehn earnestly talks to Christabel,
holding her hands, moved.
LANGBEHN: Oh, believe me, I understand your compassion. I *feel*
   it! But it is the bigger issue that must occupy our minds, day
   and night –
CHRISTABEL: Carl –
LANGBEHN: You are not a free agent! Your mercy, your

59

compassion – it threatens your husband, even your children.

CHRISTABEL: Carl – I feel ashamed –

LANGBEHN: We *are* ashamed. All of us. Shame will have to ooze out of the pores of our German skins! But – Christabel – please! Listen! You *can't* show your feelings any more than you can dare to show your thoughts! No! (*Suddenly*) God! Is that telephone pulled out of the wall!

CHRISTABEL: (*Flat*) Of course it is!

Freda quietly closes and locks the door leading to the cellar. On her way back to the kitchen, she passes by the living room.

LANGBEHN: Again and again I go to the Gestapo headquarters in the Prinz Albrechtstrasse, pitting my wits against those warped bastards. I use whatever shreds of Law are left to save the odd one here, the odd one there. I smile. I bluff. I threaten the servile shits with the names of their superiors – the higher-up swine I pretend to know intimately – God! It's degrading!

He is all but sweating, and passes a hand across his eyes, as if about to cry, then leaps up and begins pacing up and down.

CHRISTABEL: Don't. Please. Carl –

LANGBEHN: But what more can I do, *now*, a lawyer already under suspicion. It's nothing but – *gestures* . . . Miserable stop-gaps. And always wondering if my next visit will be my last. Christabel – hear me! (*Almost a shout*) It must not, will not, stop at such paltry contributions – Peter, Adam, *all* of us, are trying to play a much bigger game.

Freda hovers at the living-room door, like one not wanting to listen, but compelled to –

LANGBEHN: Christabel, you can guess how vital it is. And Christabel – Christabel – none of us can afford any *added* complications which could attract Gestapo attention! Individual compassion can compromise the very substance of much, much bigger actions.

CHRISTABEL: You didn't see her face. You didn't see the question in her eyes.

60

She is close to tears. He looks at her.

LANGBEHN: When Peter came home yesterday – What did *he* say?

CHRISTABEL: He – (*She stops.*) He said he understood.

LANGBEHN: But?

She doesn't answer, then looks away, eyes glittering.

In the hall, Freda has gone. But – the cellar door is closing: from inside.

In her bedroom, Christabel, waking, in the dark, sleepy, only gradually becomes aware that Peter is awake and brooding.

CHRISTABEL: Peter – ? What is it?

He does not move, not at once.

PETER: (*Quietly*) Nothing. I'm all right.

CHRISTABEL: Can't you tell me about it?

PETER: About what?

CHRISTABEL: About what you are doing.

Tiny pause. They are whispering.

PETER: Please. No. My love – Even if I wanted to explain, and I
     don't think I –

But he stops in mid-word. Rigid. Alert.

CHRISTABEL: Peter – ?

PETER: Shhh!

A moment. He strains to listen.

CHRISTABEL: What is it?

PETER: A noise. Downstairs.

And he is already out of bed, taking the heavy torch from the bedside table: a weapon, as well as a light.

CHRISTABEL: (*Alarmed*) Peter –

PETER: Shhh.

He is tiptoeing out.

The bright circles of the flashlight eventually illuminate a sheet of paper, laid at the foot of the stair. Peter picks it up, looks at it, then puts on the hall light.

   Christabel appears, above him, and seems to know at once what it is.

CHRISTABEL: Have they gone?

He looks up the stair at her, haunted.

PETER: Yes. They've left.

CHRISTABEL: What does it say?

PETER: They don't say why – I mean – it's from the Bible. I think.

CHRISTABEL: But where will they go? What will happen to them?

He looks at her, then reads the note.

PETER: 'The Lord is my strength and my shield; my heart hath trusted in him, and I am helped: therefore my heart –'

He stops, caught by sudden emotion. And then reads on, with narrowed throat and thickening voice.

'– therefore my heart dances for joy, and in my song will I praise him.'

They look at each other, moved, distressed.

The big clock ticks, throatily. Then –

CHRISTABEL: Will it end? Will all this ever, ever end?

PETER: (*Abrupt*) Christabel. If ever there is to be a new Germany –

But he stops, momentarily unable to get the words out, working his face with the effort of torn and conflicting emotions.

CHRISTABEL: (*Fiercely*) Then it will be built on shame!

PETER: Yes.

CHRISTABEL: (*Still fierce*) And guilt!

PETER: Yes.

She looks at him. She sees the pain.

CHRISTABEL: Oh. Peter.

PETER: (*Struggling*) But – all Germans must accept this shame – but – Chris – not all Germans must accept the guilt –

CHRISTABEL: No.

PETER: Not if they resist. If they try to *clean* – to – to –

But he has to put his hand to this throat, so tight is it, and so hard to find the right words.

CHRISTABEL: Don't.

PETER: Listen to me.

She waits. He gets command of himself. His tone changes.

I want you to go away from this city. I want you and the boys to leave Berlin.

CHRISTABEL: No!

PETER: I have things to – I have to go away for a while –

CHRISTABEL: (*Alarmed*) Why? Where?

PETER: I cannot tell you.

CHRISTABEL: Peter – ?

PETER: Please. I can't. But – that was why I was awake just now –
Chris, my love – I want you and the children out of Berlin.

CHRISTABEL: But I need you near! I can't face things without you
beside me –

PETER: Oh, darling. If it weren't for *you* I couldn't keep going. If
you weren't safe and –

He stops, because the nearest air-raid sirens start their shocking
banshee howl.

They look at each other, in distress.

Over the city, the sky is lit by searchlights. Guns pound. The
bombers above drone relentlessly, and sticks of bombs fall upon
Berlin, into already billowing smoke.

THREE

Deep into the Black Forest, a small rural steam train, huffing and puffing with slow labour, much smoke, and a single mournful whistle along a steep gradient into great bounces of wooded landscape. It is 1943, but in this fairy-tale setting, seemingly a million miles from war and distress.

Christabel, Nicholas and John in the mustily antique compartment, surrounded by their own baggage, tired out, and a bit fretful.

NICKY: Mummy?

CHRISTABEL: What is it now?

NICKY: Can I have a lollipop, please?

JOHN: Ooo! And me!

CHRISTABEL: (*Irritated*) Now how can I get a lollipop? *Where* can I get a lollipop? Come on, now – be sensible, Nicky.

John is scrambling around the carriage, bored.

JOHN: How far? Mummy? How far now – ?

CHRISTABEL: I don't know. Another hour, perhaps –

NICKY: Aw–w–w! An *hour*?

JOHN: That's a lot!

NICKY: All day! We've been in trains all the damned day!

CHRISTABEL: Don't swear!

JOHN: (*Bouncing on seat*) How far? How far *now*?

CHRISTABEL: Oh, for goodness' sake sit still for two minutes. Look out of the window or something. Look, how beautiful it is –

They press their faces against the glass, but not with any real interest.

NICKY: Yeh. Trees.

JOHN: Hills.

CHRISTABEL: (*Falsely bright*) Plenty of places to play in. No more hiding in the cellar, mmm? No more bombs. Isn't it beautiful?

NICKY: But I'd rather have a lollipop.

CHRISTABEL: Nicky!

JOHN: And me. And I would.

The country station. As the little train wheezes and expires further down the platform, the rural station master, in a red cap, talks to the only arrivals.

STATION MASTER: Berlin? By God, that's some journey that is. Berlin! That's a long old way right enough.

CHRISTABEL: You can say that again.

STATION MASTER: Must be getting rough up there? Eh? All them bombers –

CHRISTABEL: Night after night.

STATION MASTER: (*Sadly*) Aye. Looks like we got too many of 'em against us now, don't it? You think so?

Christabel, declining to answer, pretends distraction.

CHRISTABEL: How do we get to Rohrbach? Is there any sort of transport, or – ?

STATION MASTER: Rohrbach? What brings you there?

CHRISTABEL: We are evacuees. I suppose. My husband has reserved rooms for us in the village inn. He stayed there once, long ago.

STATION MASTER: Rohrbach. No. Ooh, no – No transport. Didn't he say?

CHRISTABEL: (*Exhausted*) What – ? Oh, God. Yes. He is the walking kind!

The two boys, energies newly released, have found a stack of milk churns along the platform. The churns are empty, as they discover by banging upon them.

STATION MASTER: Oh, you'll get up there, don't worry. But you'll have to wait for the milk cart. (*Looks slowly at his pocket watch.*) No more than half an hour now, I shouldn't think. They got to catch the up train to the –

CHRISTABEL: But is it far, Rohrbach?

STATION MASTER: Three, four miles up the valley. But I d'mean *up*, mind. (*Looks at her.*) Tired out, be you?

CHRISTABEL: I thought the journey would never – (*Frayed*) Nicky! John! Will you *please* stop that banging!

The station master twinkles at her, seeing her exhaustion: but also responding to her beauty.

STATION MASTER: Now, then. What about a nice cup of tea? (*At her expression*) Oh, I've managed to get my hands on some. But don't you go asking me how!

CHRISTABEL: (*Laugh*) You'll be telling me next you've got some
    lollipops.
STATION MASTER: Beg pardon?
CHRISTABEL: Tea! Oh, tea would be absolutely wonderful.

A comfortable slow old horse, driven by a comfortable, slow,
not-so-old milkman, Bausch, is pulling the milk cart up and up
into the hills.
    As the horse clip-clops, ploddingly, Bausch sings to himself the
popular German lyric of the day. Badly.
BAUSCH: (*Sings*) Bomben auf England
        Boom Boom Boom
        Whee–ee–e!
        Boom, Boom, Boom!
The sun is setting in an extravagant dazzle on the pine-fringed
ridges above and beyond.
    Finding, on the back of the cart, tucked in behind the churns,
legs dangling over the side, Christabel, Nicky and John.
    Christabel's gaze takes in the surrounding beauty and peace, to
the steady clop–clop – and her eyes start to glow. The singing is
no bother to her at all.

Clip–clop into the picture-postcard Black Forest village of
Rohrbach, with steeply sloping roofs, a steeple, and an inn,
whose sign – GASTHAUS ADLER – creaks a little in the breeze.
BAUSCH: Who–a!
A slow herd of cows is ambling past, on their daily way to pasture.
Cowbells jingling.
        (*Calls back*) Here we be! Get you down!
There are faces at the inn windows, curious, watching closely.
    Christabel and the boys get off the back of the cart. The faces
watch. Bausch sits still. But there are all their bags to get down
and carry in.
    Christabel looks around and about. The thin chimes strike on
the steeple, next to the inn. A cow moos, heavily. A long, lonely
moment. Then –
CHRISTABEL: (*Mock cheerful*) Come on, boys. All hands to the
        pump!
And then bustling out of the inn, pulling her shawl around her

66

shoulders, a stocky, late-middle-aged woman – the innkeeper
Frau Muckle comes very decidedly to the rescue.

FRAU MUCKLE: Hans! Get yourself down off that cart! Do you
    expect the lady to hump these bags by herself? Come on!
    Mo–o–ove!

Seemingly formidable, her face suddenly breaks into a warm
smile, and she extends a hand towards Christabel.

    Good day, Frau Doktor. Welcome! All the bright ones and
    all the fit ones and all the young ones have gone to the war.
    We're left with old men, cows and simpletons. And
    sometimes it's hard to tell which is which.

Christabel's laugh is primarily one of relief.

Back in the Berlin house, suitcases open on bed, Peter is packing
some things away, in the manner of one leaving this house for
ever. A sense of hurry, of tension.

CHRISTABEL'S VOICE: *My darling – even after all these weeks upon
    weeks of missing you body and soul, and so hungrily . . .*

At the inn in the Black Forest, Christabel is writing at the table in
a pretty little room with an old spinet, a green-tiled stove, and
little windows over the village street. Outside, the cowbells tinkle
past. And then the chimes from the village church. Christabel
stops writing a moment, smiles faintly.

CHRISTABEL'S VOICE: – *I still wake to the village sounds with such a
    sense of peace or even wonder –*

She resumes writing.

In Berlin, Peter going to his ramshackle car, carrying things. He
has his head down, and looks drawn, morose. Over this –

CHRISTOBEL'S VOICE: *I think the children are already less pale,
    much stronger and even more active. I go for long walks on my
    own, chattering under my breath and sometimes humming a little
    tune – guess which? –*

He puts his hands on the steering wheel, drums his fingers,
broods.

    Peter's expression changes, and Christabel's 'letter' abruptly
concludes as he hears an over-dramatic, loud squeal of brakes, as
first one and then another car pulls up in the road directly behind

him. He gets out of the car, puzzled, and with premonitions of danger.

Gestapo cars outside Langbehn's house. In each one, a driver remains. Peter, standing by his own car, examines them. A face stares back at him, with hard-eyed insolence.

Peter hesitates. He goes to the leading car. The window is already wound down.

PETER: (*To* DRIVER) What is it? What is going on?

The driver just stares. Then –

GESTAPO DRIVER: Take care of your own affairs.

About to reply, Peter sees Carl Langbehn being led out of his house by black-uniformed SS officers. He instinctively moves towards them.

PETER: Carl – !

Langbehn's swift glance at him is full of warning.

FIRST OFFICER: Get out of the way.

SECOND OFFICER: You know this man? Are you a friend of his?

Peter looks at Langbehn, whose eyes flash '*No!*'

PETER: Of course I do. He is a neighbour. What are you doing? Where are you taking –

FIRST OFFICER: (*Cutting in*) This is not your affair. Go about your business.

PETER: A good neighbour – We say good morning and we always have a drink together to celebrate the Führer's birthday – A patriot. A loyal German, and –

Langbehn smiles faintly as the SS men ignore Peter, and bundle him into the leading car.

Peter, now standing in the middle of the road, watches the cars accelerate away. His face is tight, drained. He stays completely still.

On a path in the Black Forest, Christabel crests a hill, coming along a muddy, slushy track, dressed for colder weather. She looks down upon a long slope to a small farmhouse, from near to which comes the sound of an axe, ringing as its blows cut into a felled tree.

Christabel stands completely still. Listening. Then –

CHRISTABEL'S VOICE: *My darling – I write to you all the time in my*

head, both the letters I send and the ones I cannot let you read. The
ones that tell you how sick of it all I am and how I just want to get
back amongst my own people –
Her eyes suddenly moisten, but the tears do not fall. The axe rings
as it strikes, and an echo comes back, hauntingly, from the
surrounding hills.

In Christabel's rooms at the inn, a rattle of dice, and the cube spills
out on the snakes-and-ladders board. Christabel and the two boys
are playing. John counts his way along the squares.
JOHN: Three – four – o–oooh –
He has landed on a long snake, much to Nicky's pleasure.
NICKY: Well done, snake. Good old snake.
JOHN: Shut your mouth!
CHRISTABEL: Hey – Hey! Stop that. This is a *game*. I'm still on the
     bottom line! Do *I* complain – ?
NICKY and JOHN: Yes. You do.
Christabel laughs.

Frau Muckle, the innkeeper, and Bausch, the rather simple
milkman, are approaching, in the passage and stair beyond.
FRAU MUCKLE: – And take your hat off, Hans.
BAUSCH: What?
FRAU MUCKLE: When you talk to a lady you take your hat off.
BAUSCH: Oh. Yes.
FRAU MUCKLE: Well, do it then!
She taps on the door.

CHRISTABEL: Come in!
Rattle–rattle.
     Now watch this, you two. Look at the wrist action!
Frau Muckle enters as Christabel throws a – *one*.
NICKY and JOHN: (*Derisive*) One!
FRAU MUCKLE: Ah – Aah – See that your mother don't cheat, boys.
NICKY and JOHN: She does!
CHRISTABEL: Don't say that in front of Frau Muckle – she'll throw
     me out!
FRAU MUCKLE: (*Solemn*) Never. Oh, dear God above. Never,
     Frau, dear Frau Doktor.

69

The boys are delighted by her seriousness.

CHRISTABEL: Oh, I was only –

FRAU MUCKLE: You cheat if you want to!

CHRISTABEL: (*Mock solemn*) Thank you.

FRAU MUCKLE: Please, Frau Bielenberg. Hans Bausch is at the door grinning like a fool –

BAUSCH: (*Off*) Now! Now!

FRAU MUCKLE: – And he says he has to tell you something (*Rolls her eyes*) im–por–tant.

NICKY: The milkman, Mum.

JOHN: Ice-cream!

CHRISTABEL: (*Laugh*) You'll be lucky!

FRAU MUCKLE: I don't know what's going on – Poor Hans is not too bright up top –

BAUSCH: (*Off*) Now! Now!

FRAU MUCKLE: But there's something the matter, and –

But Bausch, unwilling to be further slandered, comes half into the room, twirling his hat in his hands.

BAUSCH: Beg pardon for intrusing Frau Doktor –

FRAU MUCKLE: *Intruding!*

BAUSCH: Ay, well. Whatever it is – (*Then eagerly*) It's an American. I found I an American.

CHRISTABEL: You *what*?

FRAU MUCKLE: Hans!

BAUSCH: (*Giggle*) An American, Frau Doktor. And if you can guess what he looks like, I'll give him to you.

Christabel, of course, does not believe him, and imagines this to be some sort of childish or simple-minded game.

CHRISTABEL: Thank you very much, Hans.

Nicky and John return to the game, rattling the dice, for not even they believe it.

BAUSCH: Guess, then. Come th'on. What does he look like?

FRAU MUCKLE: Has he got a cowboy hat?

BAUSCH: Um. No. No–o.

Frau Muckle gives him a hard push.

CHRISTABEL: I know. He's wearing horn-rimmed glasses and he's smoking a big cigar.

NICKY: Oh, Mummy!

BAUSCH: No. No. Him's wearing overalls with pockets in the

knees –

FRAU MUCKLE: Hans!

BAUSCH: – and boots of right soft leather all lined wi' fur. And the stuff that his overalls be made on is as smooth as smooth as a cow's belly – !

FRAU MUCKLE: Hans Bausch. You'll get no more ale in *this* house –

But Christabel's smile has died. She stares at Hans.

JOHN: (*Excited*) A ladder! I've landed on a ladder!

NICKY: Not many rungs on it, though, are there?

CHRISTABEL: Boys. Ssshh! A minute! Go on, Hans.

FRAU MUCKLE: Oh, but –

BAUSCH: Him have got a watch too – but what a funny 'un! It's got little watches all over its face!

Christabel gets to her feet. The boys stare.

CHRISTABEL: Where did you find this – this American, Hans?

BAUSCH: Up in the trees. Lying up against my woodpile.

CHRISTABEL: And where is he now?

BAUSCH: Fast asleep.

CHRISTABEL: But where?

Frau Muckle is looking from one to the other, impressed by Christabel's seriousness, yet still not able to credit Bausch with anything other than childish mischief.

BAUSCH: Him's in my cabin. Up in the woods. I put him in, and I shut the door. (*At her steady look*) Oh 'tis true. 'Tis true!

CHRISTABEL: (*Decisive*) Nicky. John. Carry on with the game.

Nicky and John, wide-eyed now, sense exclusion.

NICKY and JOHN: Oh, Mum – !

The trees. Led by a pleased and now self-important Bausch, Christabel, the mayor, Herr Volk and a host of villagers trek higher and deeper into the dense woodland.

A log cabin, in a small clearing, like a Hansel-and-Gretel stage set. Proudly grinning, Bausch indicates the plank that locks the door, but his voice drops to a slightly comical, melodramatic whisper.

BAUSCH: I put him in there.

CHRISTABEL: Herr Bürgermeister?

71

VOLK: (*Hesitant*) Well – I – perhaps you'd better –

In the cabin, a tall, gangly-limbed young US pilot sprawls on a
rough-hewn bench against the timbered wall, heavily asleep.

CHRISTABEL: I'm awfully sorry to wake you up like this –

The pilot jerks awake and upright in almost one and the same
movement, then blinks, gasps, astonished to see a beautiful
young woman.

PILOT: Guess I'm dead. You're some kind of angel. Right?

CHRISTABEL: Sorry. No wings.

Staring at her, he expels his breath in a slow hiss.

> Are you hurt? Are you all right?

PILOT: Jeez-us.

He holds or touches his head.

CHRISTABEL: What is it – ?

PILOT: I thought I was in the Kraut's own territory –

CHRISTABEL: What?

PILOT: You're English, honey. And either I'm dreaming or –

CHRISTABEL: Look – what do you want to do? You're in the
middle of the Black Forest, and –

PILOT: The what, the black what?

CHRISTABEL: Forest.

He is suddenly very puzzled, like one dazed. But he tries a tired
sort of grin.

PILOT: Well, I'm sure glad to see *you*.

CHRISTABEL: Where were you shot down?

PILOT: I ain't the guy who knows where we're going, ma'am. We
just fly nose to tail, nose to tail. I bailed out over –
someplace. I been walking, walking. Two days and nights,
maybe –

CHRISTABEL: (*Suddenly*) England. You must have took off from
England.

PILOT: Yeh.

He looks at her, bemused.

CHRISTABEL: How are things there? How are they doing, what
does it look like?

PILOT: (*Vaguely*) England – oh, it's a nice enough little place, full
of cute little fields and – (*Then, frowning*) Why so many
questions? What's going on?

72

CHRISTABEL: But what do they think of the war – ? It's so *long* since I've been home, and – Are they all right over there? Are they managing?

PILOT: Oh. The war. (*Sudden grin*.) The war, ma'am. It's in the bag!

They look at each other. Christabel nods. Then –

CHRISTABEL: The question is – what am I going to do with you? What do you want to do?

PILOT: No problem. War's over so far as I'm concerned. I want to give myself up. I'm *tired*.

CHRISTABEL: You're sure – ?

PILOT: Hell, yes.

CHRISTABEL: Well – you stay here, right where you are, and I'll see what I can –

PILOT: (*Interrupts*.) What's your name, honey?

CHRISTABEL: Christabel.

PILOT: That's *nice*. Christabel, honey – no kidding. This is it, right? Germany.

CHRISTABEL: Germany.

He sighs wearily, stretches out again. Then –

PILOT: Chris–ta–bel. That's a real nice name.

He falls asleep, abruptly, like a light going out.

Christabel contemplates him with a small smile, and rehearses his phrase.

CHRISTABEL: 'It's in the bag.'

In the main room of the inn, the American pilot, ravenously hungry, sits at a long bare wood table digging into a large hunk of dark, rough bread, some cold meat on the bone, a chunk of crumbling cheese and some wine from an earthenware pitcher. It is as though he has not eaten for a week.

But as he wipes his mouth with the back of his hand, the first fierce pangs assuaged, he gradually (and comically) becomes aware that he is being observed with an untoward intensity.

Standing well away from the table, virtually against the walls, Volk, Sepp, Alois, Frau Muckle, Nicky, John, Christabel and a few others are examining him with the same order of fascination that they might show if they were watching an exotic animal at its watering hole.

Christabel smiles across at him, to reassure him. He ill-suppresses a sudden and unexpected burp.

PILOT: Ooops. Beg pardon.

Instantly, there is a murmur of whispers around Christabel.

VOLK, FRAU MUCKLE and SEPP: (*Sotto voce*) What did he say? What was that – ?

CHRISTABEL: He said that it was very nice. The food.

Frau Muckle beams with pleasure, and rather nervously goes across to the table.

FRAU MUCKLE: Some more wine? Yes?

He blinks at her, getting more and more puzzled by such interest, such kindness.

PILOT: Thank you, ma'am.

As he drinks, he becomes aware of yet another level of observation – for there are faces pressed all but flat against the glass of the small windows of the inn, street side, peering in at him with the same unnerving intensity.

Increasingly self-conscious, he goes on eating and drinking. Christabel suppresses a private smile of a genuine hilarity.

The railway station in Berlin now shows a much more war-worn atmosphere than before, as an arriving train disgorges mostly uniformed passengers.

Christabel, alone, arriving with a small bag, looks up and down – but there is no one to meet her. She stands. She waits.

News placards announce the Normandy landings: 'The fortress is attacked' and 'Invasion of European fortress' and, starkly, 'Invasion!'

In her Berlin flat, Lexi gives tired and troubled Christabel coffee.

LEXI: I *think* it's made out of acorns but – well, pretend it's coffee. It's hot, anyway.

CHRISTABEL: Bless you, Lexi, I've been walking around for hours – and when I finally got to the old house, I just couldn't bear to go in. I felt – absolutely lost. Totally bereft.

LEXI: You need a compass to get across Berlin now – Night after night it's a hell hole – and all it does is make people – (*She stops, shrugs.*) Your journey can't have been much fun.

CHRISTABEL: I hadn't heard from Peter in so long – I tried to telephone. Nothing. So I sent a postcard to say –

LEXI: (*Abrupt*) Keep away, Christabel! Keep out of it!

Christabel stares at her. Then –

CHRISTABEL: Lexi. Where is Peter?

LEXI: Go back, Christabel. By the first train you can get. He's all
    right. Adam's all right. But what has to be done has to be
    done.

A beat. Christabel puts her cup down.

CHRISTABEL: What do you mean?

Lexi looks at her. Then smiles. Then –

LEXI: Christabel, darling. Would you like something to eat? I
    haven't got much here, but – you can always get hold of
    something if you know how.

And she abruptly leaves the room.

    Christabel stares into nothingness, weary, worried, puzzled.
She gets up. She sits down again. Then, unbearably tense now,
she goes to the door, opens it, and sees –

Lexi is not preparing food, she is on the telephone, listening. She
turns and looks at Christabel, expressionless, then –

LEXI: (*On phone*) Yes. She will be there. Look out for us.

Christabel and Lexi sit on a bench in the station concourse, too
distant for their apparently earnest conversation to be heard.
    Adam arrives, looks around, and his eyes pick out and settle
upon them. He smiles, but does not move towards them
immediately.

The same bench, a little later, with only Christabel and Adam. He
holds her hand, reassuringly.

ADAM: I don't know whether anyone outside now believes there is
    another Germany. We have tried to talk to the Allies, but –
    Chris. That chapter is closed. From now on this is a German
    affair. No one else will help. We must rid ourselves – alone.

She all but shudders.

CHRISTABEL: (*Almost whisper*) How? But – oh, how?

ADAM: Believe me, it will be done. It will and must be done.
    Everything is ready, and in place. (*Quickly*) Don't ask more.
    Don't say more. I have already told you too much.

She goes to speak, and then doesn't. He smiles, but then is distracted by a battalion of soldiers being marched to a train. They seem to be mostly old men. His face clouds.

CHRISTABEL: Adam – ?

ADAM: Can't help feeling bad when I see old men like that in uniform. Me in my Sunday best.

CHRISTABEL: Don't say that!

ADAM: I'd make a rotten soldier.

CHRISTABEL: But you're a fighter for something far bigger than those stamping boots and uniforms and – (*Upset, she has to stop.*) Please. Try, try to take care. And if you see Peter, tell him – tell him –

ADAM: Yes. I know. And I will.

They look at each other. A corporal shouts an order, off.

CHRISTABEL: Adam. God bless you. And God protect you in whatever it is you are trying to do.

He inclines his head with a graceful smile, then kisses her cheek, and stands.

ADAM: One day this nightmare will end – you'll see. One day we shall breathe clean air again. Goodbye Christabel.

She watches him go, her eyes glistening. Before he goes out of sight, he turns and lifts his hand.

Back in the Black Forest, the village inn sign creaks in the slight wind, and the little church bing–bongs its thin chime.

Christabel lies sleepless within the inn, in half-light.

PETER'S VOICE: *Darling, my darling, I beg you to be patient a little while. Never imagine for one moment that there is an echoless void where love should be – and duty too.*

She clicks on her lamp, and reads the bit that worries her again in the letter on the bedside table.

Darling. Great changes may be coming very soon. Be awake!

A moment. Then, tense, she gets up, lifts the latch on the adjoining door, looks in at –

Nicky and John fast asleep in the tiny room.

She quietly closes their door, stands still a moment.

PETER'S VOICE: *Great changes may be coming very soon. Be awake!*

Daytime in the village street. Tinkle–tinkle of cowbells as the herd plods by on its way to pasture.

Then, from the top end of the single street, the old man Alois comes running towards the inn, yelling his head off.

ALOIS: Turn on the wireless! Turn on the wireless! They've thrown a bomb at Hitler! Turn on the wireless!

Windows squeaking open. Heads popping out.

Christabel wakes with a start, then the sense of what is being shouted in the street below smacks her, all at once.

She looks at Peter's letter at her bedside. Quickly, with a catch of breath, she grabs it up, crumpling it into her hand. She crosses to the stove, and sets light to the letter with a match, holding it long enough in her hand to ensure that the flame engulfs it, then dropping it into the empty stove.

Then realizes that Nicky is staring at her from his opened door.

NICKY: Mum?

CHRISTABEL: Quickly. Get dressed.

Later. The small inn is so crowded that some villagers are standing at the door, jostling close.

Mayor Volk is addressing everybody, speaking against a hubbub, and standing on the table.

VOLK: All I can say is – all I can say – As the Mayor, I have made my call to Herr Inspector in Furtwangen, who had to call the Inspector in Donaueschingen –

FRAU MUCKLE: And who did he call?

Some laughter. Volk raises his hand.

VOLK: The Führer is alive and well. The bomb did not harm him.

BAUSCH: Thank goodness. Thank the Lord.

Heads turn in his direction.

VOLK: The Inspector in Donaueschingen told the Inspector in Furtwangen –

ALOIS: Who told the bell.

VOLK: Listen! I – oh, stop the noise! There is to be broadcast at noon – We all have to stop whatever we are doing and pay attention!

The long corridor at the ministry in Berlin is the same expanse Adam ran along before, but now he walks along it, in the midst of marching, black-garbed SS officers.

It is a long walk, the boots thundering and echoing on the marble. A few people half open their office doors, looking out, in mixed fear and sympathy, and very occasionally in triumph or pleasure.

RADIO VOICE: – *attempted coup on the life of the beloved Führer has failed utterly and miserably. The traitors and renegades responsible are even now being apprehended in their funk-holes –*

In the Berlin streets air-raid sirens howl, and the few people on the pavements are running for the shelters.

A Gestapo car sweeps by, at speed –

In the back, tightly between menacing figures, Peter, grim faced as the car sweeps through an archway and into a darkening yard.

RADIO VOICE: – *and will be sentenced in the manner they deserve. German Men! German Woman! Do not grieve! The Führer is unharmed –*

In Rohrbach the cows are coming back from pasture, ambling in their slow, heavy-uddered way into the village street –

RADIO VOICE: – *and he has announced to a grateful nation, in his own voice, in his own unmistakable historic tones, at this hour of destiny for our people, that Providence has saved him for a glorious task. Heil Hitler!*

Sound of 'Deutschland über Alles' being played, on radio.

But the anthem, and the placid cows, overborne by the shatteringly noisy arrival of motorcycle-and-sidecar, bumping up the steep track, scattering the animals in fear, and making the herdsman shout and gesticulate.

Is it the police?

At the inn, the mayor, Herr Volk, hat twisting in his hands, is not quite able to look Christabel in the eye, and stands half out of the doorway.

VOLK: And he said, that fellow, that man from Donaueschingen,

78

that you – um – (*He coughs, embarrassed.*) You are not
allowed to leave the village, Frau Doktor Bielenberg. He –
that fellow – he asked us all about you. The man from
Donaueschingen. My God! I mean – well!

He waits, darts her a look, darts his eyes away again.

CHRISTABEL: What sort of things did he ask, Herr Volk? And
    why?

Her voice is controlled, but she is stiff with tension. She senses
'why'.

VOLK: Oh – um – whether you talked politics at all, or – I can
    assure you I gave you a great reference! I told him you didn't
    have an idea in your head. (*Swallow.*) About *politics*, I mean,
    pardon, Frau Doktor.

Frau Muckle, concentrating, face full of indignation, strains to
listen, below.

VOLK: I told him how you worked with the villagers picking
    stones off the potato patch, and how – well, how your boys
    helped with the herding. And that. All that. I am not
    supposed to tell you this – he said we would be shot if we told
    you anything except about being kept to the village – stupid
    Lowlander! If you want to go to Furtwangen or any place to
    do some shopping, just let me know, that's all – God
    Almighty!

CHRISTABEL: (*With difficulty*) Did he – please, Herr Volk, my
    Husband. Did he say –

She stops, scared of the question. He shuffles a bit, then whispers
in hoarse dread, his hand flying to his mouth –

VOLK: He is in prison, Frau Doktor. The man from
    Donaueschingen said I was not to –

CHRISTABEL: (*Cries out*) What for! Did he say what for!

Volk turns to go, head down.

VOLK: (*Mumble*) I don't know as – I –

CHRISTABEL: Please!

He stops, and looks back at her.

VOLK: High treason.

He shuts the door behind him, hurriedly.
    Christabel holds herself stiff and still and quiet.

Frau Muckle upbraids a retreating, embarrassed Volk as he passes through the tap room.

FRAU MUCKLE: Picking stones off the potato patches! Is that all you could think of! Potatoes! What's that on top of your shoulders, then? Hey? Are you a potato as well!

Above, Christabel remains still and silent, like one in shock. Then, suddenly released, she cries out, a single noise of anguish. And stops herself.

Nicky has opened the adjoining door. He stands for a moment looking at her, in his pyjamas, before she is aware of it. Then –

NICKY: Is Daddy dead?

Christabel starts. She looks at him, at his solemnly anxious face.

CHRISTABEL: No, he is not. He is in prison.

NICKY: In *prison*? Daddy in prison? But *why* – ?

Christabel hesitates.

CHRISTABEL: Some – some enemies of his have told stories, and – Wicked people have got Daddy into trouble. His enemies.

NICKY: But what about the police! Mummy – if people have told lies about Daddy, the police will find out and let him out, won't they?

CHRISTABEL: Well. (*Quickly*) Yes! Yes! of course!

But he is looking at her intently.

NICKY: When this war is over, I don't want to stay in Germany.

CHRISTABEL: (*Quietly*) No.

NICKY: I want to go back to England. I want to be English, Mummy! Mummy – do you hear? I want to be English!

He is starting to cry, but holds it back.

Ravensbrück. As seen through a slit in a cell wall in the block, narrowed down, a yard below.

Some women prisoners with shaven heads, propped up against the wall, are being whipped mercilessly. It is a punishment wall.

In his cell, Peter whirls away from the slit he has been looking through, trembling with rage and disgust. His hands are chained.

He crouches in the corner, in a foetal position, trying to stop his ears to the terrible sounds coming from below, sucking in his breath.

In Rohrbach, the little village children sing 'Silent Night'.

The snow has come, making the village seem like a Christmas card.
The 'Heilige Nacht' coming through the windows, high, sweet and clear.

The 'Heilige Nacht' continuing to the execution shed, in Berlin.
Adam, haggard, his arms strapped behind his back, looks at the noose on a butcher's hook.
To both the right and left of it, bodies gently swing.
A movie camera is being operated in the corner of the room, making a whirring noise.
He is led on to a crate under his own noose.

In the village school, the pupils (including Nicky and John) reaching the end of the carol.
Christabel, her eyes on her boys, sits with Frau Muckle, and Volk. Alois, twinkling proudly at the singers, plays the tinny piano.

Night in the village. Moonlight on snow, and the creak of the inn sign.

The alarm clock jangles in Christabel's room in the inn. Her arm shoots out to stifle it. The hands show 3 a.m. as she clicks on her lamp.
Christabel forces herself out of bed. She is already fully dressed under the cover.
She first goes to the adjoining door to look in. The boys are asleep.

Frau Muckle, a shawl over her flannel nightdress, is at the stove as Christabel comes down.
CHRISTABEL: (*Surprised*) Frau Muckle – what are you – ?
FRAU MUCKLE: You're not going all that terrible long way
    without something inside you! You're going to need all your
    strength if –
She dumps a plate of hot food on to the table.

CHRISTABEL: (*Moved*) I'll never forget your kindness –
FRAU MUCKLE: Eat! Never mind Never! When you find your
     husband he won't want to see skin-and-bone!
Frau Muckle, bustling about, gets a tin down from the shelf.
CHRISTABEL: Oh – no! You mustn't – !
But she has opened the lid, and taken out two or at most three
coffee beans.
FRAU MUCKLE: Just a few little beans! A little cup of *real* coffee.
     This is what it's for – a special day!

Bausch, muffled, heavily yawning, arrives with horse and sleigh
at the inn.

Inside, Christabel is heaving on a rucksack.
CHRISTABEL: The letter to my parents –
FRAU MUCKLE: Well hid! And their address is in the cocoa tin
     under the redcurrant bush – Hey – it won't be needed! God
     will take care of you! And if they let you see your husband –
     tell him – tell him –
CHRISTABEL: Now, now, no tears, dear Frau Muckle. I'll be
     back! But I can't tell you what it means to me to be able to
     leave the children in your care. Please! Spoil them a little!
They embrace, each with brimming eyes, as Bausch clatters and
boot-thumps into the kitchen from the main room beyond.

Distant mountains white in the pre-dawn sky, and the sleigh
gliding and jingling, with Bausch and Christabel, blanket
covered.

The Berlin-bound train, thundering north through a snowy land.

Every square inch within the train seems crowded, mostly with
soldiers.
   Finding in the packed carriages and loaded corridors
Christabel, with her rucksack used as a rest, uncomfortably and
wearily propped in the corridor.
   Some soldiers eye her lasciviously, but her expression has not
changed, her eyes fixed ahead, her thoughts blank.

At Ravensbrück Camp, hands chained, Peter shuffles with other prisoners on 'exercise', his eyes darting, examining everything.

Klaxons start to blare, harshly, from the camp beyond.

On the crowded train, a wiry little Berliner, squad comedian, has been drawing out Christabel.

BERLIN SOLDIER: Run? Never so fast in me life! Ever see an army on the run? Eh?

CHRISTABEL: No.

BERLINER: Once an army starts running, there's nothing as'll stop them. Not even a pretty girl like you.

FIRST SOLDIER: (*Wink*) Oh, I don't know –

BERLINER: First we threw away our drinking bottles, then our helmets, belts, ammunition – and then our rifles. Gawd! I can see them chasing us now –

SECOND SOLDIER: Just as we popped over one hill they got to the top of the one behind us –

THIRD SOLDIER: Boom! Bo–oo–oom!

BERLINER: One thing I can tell you, Fräulein. I'm not trying for no Iron Cross!

FOURTH SOLDIER: Don't worry, Heini – You won't get one neither!

BERLINER: No – and I don't want a wooden one! When this little lot's over I'm going back to me vegetable stall. Me–lons! (*Looks at her with a gleam.*) I misses me melons. Ripe melons.

The others laugh at his sexual innuendo.

But this is cut short by a violent jerk of train as its brakes are abruptly applied, throwing them all together.

SECOND SOLDIER: (*Indifferent*) Oh God – a raid, I expect.

BERLIN SOLDIER: If they want to hit any more targets, they'll have to bring them with them.

The dark hulk of the train, stopped on the approaches to a town that is being raided.

In the distance, searchlights slicing the sky, anti-aircraft batteries pounding away, the drone of bombers above.

On the train, bodies pressed close, faces gleaming in the dark, baby crying somewhere, sounds of the air raid in the near distance.

83

BERLIN SOLDIER: (*No rancour*) Heathen bastards. Don't they
know it's Christmas? You think they'd give us a bit of a
break, eh?

SOLDIER: Here's to that! Christmas at home.

The Berliner starts to sing, in a surprisingly beautiful voice, the
most haunting of all German soldier songs.

BERLIN SOLDIER: (*Sings*) In der Heimat

    In der Heimat
    Da Gibt's ein Wiedersehen
    In the homeland
    In the homeland
    There we shall meet again –

The other soldiers take up the words, and soon it seems as though
the whole train is filling with the sad, wistful song.

Beyond the searchlights of the town, the train is a dark snake,
immobile. The song swells, sentimental and insistent.

The morning, and the train clank–clanks slowly towards a station
approach, where lines of abused Slav prisoners are clearing piles
of rubble.

BERLIN SOLDIER: If they do one half to us of what we've done to
them –

He falls silent. The others stare out of the frost-patterned
windows.

The soldiers crowd off the train, calling, 'Happy Christmas'.
   The Berliner, getting on to the platform, looks up at
Christabel, clicks his heels, raises his right arm, squaring small
shoulders.

BERLIN SOLDIER: Well, whoever still wants to listen, *Heil Hitler*,
et cetera, et ceter–*a*!

Christabel swallows her laugh as a man glares, brushing past her
to the open door.

Later. Christabel has now managed to get a seat in the carriage.
She shivers in the corner, hunching into herself, and stares
bleakly out at the scudding winter landscape.

A yellow and black notice opposite her, at rack level, says
BEWARE! AN ENEMY MAY BE LISTENING!

Later. Christabel waking, cold in near darkness, as the train again
jerks to a rough stop. She blinks, not quite sure for a moment
where she is, and, focusing on the sign –
    BEWARE! AN ENEMY MAY BE LISTENING!
    And next to it, a black-peaked army cap, decorated with the
skull and crossbones of the SS, in a sudden illumination, for –

A searchlight is sweeping upwards from just beside the track,
momentarily shining through the window, throwing everything
into brilliant relief – including –
    A tall figure in black, with forked-lightning insignia,
motionless, eyes fixed on Christabel. Exactly like an image
illuminated in nightmare.
    The beam slides on upwards, taking with it Christabel's gasp.
    Semi-darkness suddenly. Sounds of air raid, near.
SS MAN: (*Softly*) You have been asleep.
CHRISTABEL: (*Shiver*) I – yes – wh – what is – Where are we?
SS MAN: We are just outside Berlin, Fräulein. There is a raid. The
    train must wait for the British to evacuate their bowels.
Christabel realizes they are alone in the compartment. She
involuntarily shivers, from cold, and the lingering shock.
    Would you like my greatcoat over your knees? It is very cold.
CHRISTABEL: N–no, thank you –
He smiles coldly.
SS MAN: We have the compartment to ourselves. Do you know
    why?
CHRISTABEL: I – sorry? –
SS MAN: For the same reason you reject my coat.
She is silent. Then, bravely –
CHRISTABEL: Perhaps. Yes.
The horizon is lit by bombs, flames, searchlights.
SS MAN: (*Softly*) We could be waiting, could we not, on the
    outskirts of Hell?
She is silent, but, in this weird half-light, her eyes are helplessly
drawn to his pale, slightly twitching face.
    I am from Riga. Do you know of Riga?

She doesn't want to talk.

CHRISTABEL: Latvia.

SS MAN: Our people baked cakes and stood by the roadside and gave them to the German troops as they marched through our villages. We were so glad. Our Russian Occupation had been very hard. They killed my father, for instance. My mother died of grief.

POOM! POOM! POOM! outside, from the ack-ack batteries.

   Christabel stares at the black-uniformed Latvian, almost like one hypnotized by his soft, matter-of-fact, yet strangely insistent voice.

CHRISTABEL: (*Swallow*) War is a terrible –

SS MAN: (*Same tones*) The troops looked so – splendid. My only wish in the world was to join them, and take my revenge for what the Russians had done to my home. I had the correct Aryan measurements, so I had the particular honour of being recruited for the SS.

CHRISTABEL: I – I'm rather tired, and –

It is as though she has not spoken. His eyes are fixed straight ahead, and his body remains stiff, his voice hypnotically, insistently soft, almost caressingly so.

SS MAN: They told us we could revenge ourselves on our enemies. But do you know what we did? We killed Jews. We just had the shooting to do. Others did the burying.

Silence. She stares. His eyes have not shifted. Then they do, focusing clear on her, yet oddly 'far off'.

   Do you know what it means? To kill Jews. Men, women and children as they stand in a semi-circle around the machine-guns?

CHRISTABEL: *What?*

SS MAN: There was a little boy. He stood there to attention. And he asked me, 'Do I stand straight enough, Uncle?' Yes. He asked that of me. And once, once when the circle stood around us, an old man stepped out of the ranks. Long hair. Beard. One of their priests, I suppose. He stopped within a few feet of the guns. He looked at us. He looked at each and every one of us, straight at us. Deep into us. I will never forget it. But I hope there is not much time left in which to – remember.

Silence, except for the raid on Berlin, beyond. Christabel cannot move, cannot speak. He looks out of the window, just once, then back at her, and then begins again, in the same low monotone.

>'My children,' he said. 'My children. God is watching what you do.'

His eyes suddenly flare and burn, though it may be from a sudden change in the light outside, due to the bombardment.

>We shot them.

He stares. She has to press her knuckles against her mouth.

>His face goes dead. He looks out of the window. BANG! CRASH!

>Then, in what is almost a whisper of awe, he repeats

>'My children. God is watching what you do.'

Silence. He turns again, and stares at her.

In Berlin, rubble is piled on either side of the diminished roadway, and some of the heaps have small wooden crosses on them, to show bodies buried beneath.

>Christabel, looking about, and picking an uncertain way forward, with her rucksack on her back, sees a small Christmas tree and Nativity crib in the ruins.

>Upset, she turns around and about, lost, unable to find any familiar landmark.

>Ahead of her, some people are cooking vegetables on a small oil stove in the rubble, near to a telephone kiosk, standing surrealistic in the acres of desolation.

No matter how bizarre, the fact is that the telephone in the kiosk is working.

CHRISTABEL: (*On phone*) This is the Dahlemer Laundry. I am speaking from a call-box. I know you are on the Budapesterstrasse, but I cannot find my way to your house – Would you mind coming down to fetch your washing – ? Ah. Yes. I see. The third pile of rubble –

Back on the ruined streets, an irate woman calls across from a hole in the rubble.

IRATE WOMAN: You seen my bloody dustbin, Frau? It was here a minute ago.

CHRISTABEL: Sorry. No –

IRATE WOMAN: It's any excuse nowadays – ! What's it all coming to, eh?

Disappearing back into her hole, as Christabel picks her way foward.

Lexi is standing there, in the rubble, waiting for Christabel. Her eyes flash warningly.

LEXI: (*Loudly*) Heil Hitler, meine dame!

CHRISTABEL: Heil Hitler. Would it be possible for us to – There are things missing in your laundry, you see . . .

LEXI: Such a bore, isn't it? Bombs. But they say it won't be long before our leader has another brainwave –

CHRISTABEL: Pray God!

LEXI: Some sort of wonder weapon! That'll sort 'em out! But let me show you my cosy little abode – I'm not going to discuss missing underwear in the street, thank you very much.

Unexpected faces look out from unexpected places, as they traverse what were doorways, windows, half-flight of stairs, and across what was obviously an inner court, reaching –

Lexi's crumbling flat.

LEXI: Recognize the hall – That's the sitting room as well. No wall. Here's my bedroom – pretty good, eh? But if you open *that* door you'll fall straight to kingdom come. And look – *a telephone* – Isn't that crazy? They actually came round and mended it!

She is almost gabbling – then stops, tears trembling.

CHRISTABEL: (*Moved*) Lexi.

LEXI: (*Brutally*) They hanged Adam. They hanged him slowly. They hanged him from a meat hook.

Christabel sucks in her breath, sways. Lexi grabs her forearm.

CHRISTABEL: I'm I'm –

LEXI: Sit down. Sit down!

CHRISTABEL: Lexi – I can't bear – Lexi. What about Peter? Peter.

LEXI: He's in Ravensbrück concentration camp.

Now Christabel sits – like a dead weight.

Later, at her flat, Lexi throws a chair leg into the stove.

LEXI: – If. If. If the bomb had not been moved under Hitler's
   table – No – darling – you must stay without dangerous
   knowledge if you are going to do this – (*Suddenly*) Why don't
   they *come*? Why don't the British, the Americans – Listen.
   One of our people has got a job in the reception office at
   Ravensbrück. He saw Peter three days ago. He was able to
   say one sentence. 'Non-Political.'
CHRISTABEL: (*Tensing*) Non-Political.
LEXI: Keep it in front of you all the time, no matter what.
   Non-political. That's how he's holding out under
   interrogation. You can be sure Adam took his secrets with
   him. Chris – oh, Chris! They took pictures of them while
   they hanged them.
She covers her face.

At the station (Berlin) a brass band playing German Christmas
music in a damaged concourse – at the moment, 'Süsser die
Glocken nie klingen'.
   Christabel and Lexi talk quietly on a bench, huddled.
LEXI: Most of his friends are dead and can't give evidence against
   him. We've got *that* through! And remember – these Gestapo
   are not all wise and knowing. They can be pretty stupid – I
   mean, what sort of person would want to –
She stops. An SS soldier sits too close. He is interested in them,
but only as attractive women.
   Christabel and Lexi light cigarettes and move away. The soldier
watches them, shifts, and sighs.

The band, mostly old men, and boys, begin to play 'O
Tannenbaum'.

In the waiting room, at the station, fully kitted soldiers crowd.
Lexi and Christabel at a corner table, where two soldiers slump,
asleep.
LEXI: (*Quietly urgent*) Listen – some of the rats have enough sense
   to be frightened out of their filthy skins – Talk about your
   connections in England. Who is that uncle of yours, Lord
   whosit – ?
CHRISTABEL: Rothermere.

LEXI: What's he do?

CHRISTABEL: Newspapers.

LEXI: What's he do on them?

CHRISTABEL: Own them.

A beat. Then they both laugh – and are glad to do so. Then Lexi grips Christabel's wrist.

LEXI: By the time you get there, your appointment will be
     arranged. I hope! (*Then*) Are you sure you can do this?

Christabel looks at her. It is answer enough.

     We know his interrogator. We know what he is. A frightened
     piece of filth – Lange – L–a–n–g–e –

One of the sleeping soldiers stirs, half wakes. Lexi stops, abruptly.

   The soldier stares at them blearily for a moment, then makes a crude kissing sound with his lips – and goes straight back to sleep, head on arms. Lexi stares, then –

     Who would this Lord whatsit know in the British
     Government? *Christabel* – say anything! Promise anything!
     It's your only chance!

Christabel looks at her, and nods.

The branch-line train rocks along the plain, where snow makes everything look the same, and Christabel stares out through the frosty patterns on the window.

   In the carriage, a woman with two children, both girls. She is reading a box, and the girls are eating sweets.

   But Christabel has no eyes for them at the moment, self-absorbed, gazing sightlessly through the carriage window, rehearsing, in her mind –

CHRISTABEL'S VOICE: *I owe you gratitude, Herr Kriminalrat Lange.*
     It is good of you to give me some of your valuable time –

One of the little girls, a sweet in her mouth, swinging her legs, starts to sing, tunelessly.

MOTHER: Don't sing with your mouth full, Edeltraut!

The little girl stops at once. And Christabel, momentarily distracted, resumes her thoughts –

CHRISTABEL'S VOICE: *Of course, Herr – um – Herr Lange, I*
     have total – absolute – confidence in German Justice – and –
     and –

She sighs, hating it, and her eyes wander around the compartment.

EDELTRAUT: I want a biscuit.

MOTHER: Oh. All right. You've not stopped eating since we left –

The other little girl, mouth full of toffee, wants some too.

HILDE: And me, And me, And me.

The mother sighs, takes down a case, takes out a big bag of biscuits.

MOTHER: Count yourself lucky, you two. *Most* people are not so
    lucky nowadays –

A quick glance at Christabel, who looks away, controlling her enmity.

EDELTRAUT: *Their* daddies are not so imp–or–tant, that's why!

MOTHER: Don't speak with your mouth full.

HILDE: Why is Daddy –

She has to stop to chew–chew–crunch–crunch a bulging cheekful of biscuit.

    Why is Daddy all the way down here – Mum? Why is –

MOTHER: (*Trying to read*) Because the Fatherland needs him. Be
    quiet, will you? For five minutes.

Christabel's gaze is back on them. And then her expression freezes as she sees –

A tag-tied label, swinging on the mother's case, disturbed when the bag of biscuits was removed, with a single name: LANGE.

Christabel examines the three with more interest.

    Crunch–crunch–chew–chew from the two dreadful little girls.

    Edeltraut's jaws stop working a moment as she becomes conscious of Christabel's gaze. And the nasty child covertly puts out her tongue. Christabel waits for the right moment, and then does it back.

Eventually, Christabel looks through the lace patterns of frost on the train window to see the word RAVENSBRÜCK on the small wooden station, set in the middle of a white nowhere.

    The woman and her daughters stand.

MOTHER: Wipe your mouth, Hilde. There are crumbs. What will
    people think of you?

EDELTRAUT: Will there be a car?
MOTHER: Of course!
HILDE: I feel sick.
MOTHER: Oh – you *would*! Come on. Hurry up.
HILDE: (*Wail*) Mum! I feel sick!
But they are getting out. Christabel, waiting, watching, has
narrowed eyes, full of hostility.

Christabel is trudging along a straight and featureless road
through a flat and bleak land, towards the camp. The wind howls
as it tears at her.
    She does not hear the big black Mercedes as it comes up behind
her, sporting Nazi insignia. As the car rushes towards her, it
hoots loudly, at almost the last possible moment, and she has to
jump out of its way. Sweeping past, its wheels send up a slurry of
mud, all over her. And grinning at her through the back
window are the two dreadful little girls.
    Christabel stands still a moment, dripping, and trying to digest
the indignity of it, and her rage.
    Then, back in control, and with what is almost a smile, she
trudges on and on into the featureless desolation, a lone
woman bending into the wind, with a voice in her head saying –
LEXI'S VOICE: *Christabel – say anything! Promise anything! It's
    your only chance.*

FOUR

Out of a bleak and featureless nowhere, Christabel, trudging on
and on towards the camp perimeters – remembering –
LEXI'S VOICE: *By the time you get there, darling, we will have
arranged your appointment. I hope. If you're sure you can do it.
If you're sure . . .*
She lifts her head and sees, ghostly, half-silhouetted in front of
her – the watchtowers.

Beginning to quail a little, cold, very dispirited, Christabel
approaches.
LEXI'S VOICE: *We know his interrogator. We know what he is. A
frightened piece of filth.*
Glancing up as she passes under the first tower, Christabel sees
that the guard in his sheepskins is aiming a tommy gun right at
her. Her step falters.
    But the bored guard is (sort of) joking. He grins broadly. And
then whistles at her, would-be lascivious, peering out between the
flaps of his fur collar.
    Christabel trudges on, set-faced, passing several more towers
and hundreds of yards of barbed wire.

She reaches a red, white and black barrier. A sheepskinned,
ear-flapped, armed guard points her towards a long narrow
wooden hut at the entrance.
    Bracing herself, she goes in –
LEXI'S VOICE: *Christabel. Say anything! Promise anything! It's your
only chance!*

In the reception hut, portraits of Hitler, Heydrich,
Kaltenbrunner on the walls, with black ribbon on the Heydrich
picture, because he is dead.
    At the far end, two huge flags cover the wall: the swastika, and
the regimental colours of the SS. In front of them, a desk, at
which sits a mild-faced, elderly, tired-looking clerk, coping with
inquiries.

There are many visitors, some leaving, most sitting in patient postures at benches around the walls, and a line of them in front of the desk.

At the desk, a young Wehrmacht officer seems to be pleading with the clerk.

OFFICER: – all right, all right, it wasn't very sensible of me, I know. But – look – please – I have to leave for the Russian front tonight. So I thought in the circumstances –

CLERK: (*Not unsympathetic*) But you have no appointment.

OFFICER: It's my *father* –

CLERK: I know. I know. I'm – But think about it. It's obviously not possible for people to turn up out of the blue and just walk in and talk to a prisoner, now is it?

OFFICER: How could I have made an appointment? I've been at the front. And I've only got a three-day pass – (*He clutches his little parcel into his chest.*) And I wanted him to have this.

CLERK: What is that? What have you got there?

OFFICER: Cigarettes. Some cigarettes.

CLERK: Oh, dear. I feel very – (*To* CHRISTABEL) Yes?

CHRISTABEL: I have an appointment to see Herr Kriminalrat Lange –

CLERK: (*Brusque*) Name!

CHRISTABEL: Christabel Bielenberg.

His expression changes. It is almost as though he looks at her with a gleam of understanding. He controls it.

CLERK: Sit down over there, please. And wait to be called. (*To* YOUNG OFFICER) Now – I don't suppose it will do you much good, but I'll telephone through and see if –

Christabel goes to a bench. As she sits, some departing visitors come through a far door, escorted by an armed guard. They look frightened, or shocked, and one old woman is weeping, stuffing a handkerchief tight against her mouth.

The young officer sits near to Christabel, to wait. He catches her sympathetic eye, shifts a bit, slightly embarrassed.

OFFICER: I – um – I don't know whether to be depressed or angry. Neither do much good, do they?

CHRISTABEL: Did I hear you say you have to go back to your unit tonight?

OFFICER: Yes.

CHRISTABEL: But – couldn't you miss the train, and sit it out – ?
OFFICER: (*Shocked*) What – ?
CHRISTABEL: (*Quickly*) Some official might come through and
    give you a permit after all, you see –
OFFICER: Miss the train? But my leave is up!
CHRISTABEL: Oh. Yes. I – ah – Yes. But if they won't let you see
    your father before you go back to the – (*Carefully*) Doesn't it
    make you wonder a little what it is you are fighting for?
He is looking at her in an almost childlike, shocked
bewilderment.
OFFICER: I am fighting for Germany.
CHRISTABEL: Yes. Of course. I –
And only then, as though he finally understands her question –
OFFICER: For Germany – (*Gestures at the flags.*) Not for all that
    stuff. For Germany.
CLERK: (*Calls*) Frau Doktor Bielenberg. If you please.
As she stands, the young officer jumps to his feet, and shakes
hands with her.
OFFICER: Good luck to you, gnädige Frau.
CHRISTABEL: And to you, too!
OFFICER: I assure you it is no penance to go back to the front.
    The air is cleaner there.
CLERK: (*Calls*) Frau Bielenberg!

Led by a silent, armed SS guard, an apprehensive Christabel
crosses a parade ground where SS guards drill to sharp staccato
commands.
    Beyond, behind more barbed wire, and under yet more
watchtowers, is the first compound, full of shuffling prisoners,
chained at the hand, on exercise.
    Christabel is all eyes, peering anxiously, hopefully across, but,
at too brisk a pace –
    They reach and enter an administration block, where there are
more guards.

Christabel sits waiting in a long room with grey light coming
through the windows, beneath which are yellow desks, at which
sit women at typewriters.
    Opposite the women, four prisoners, heavily chained hand and

foot, sitting necessarily awkwardly, an armed guard behind them.

Soft, low, indecipherable murmurs, and louder clack–clack of typewriters, as the prisoners dictate statements or confessions, clear signs of physical abuse about their faces, their postures.

At the desk nearest her, a sudden loud voice all but makes her jump. It comes from the young hard-faced blonde at the typewriter.

BLONDE WOMAN: Haven't you finished yet!

PRISONER: No – nearly. I've –

He is reading over his statement, page after page.

BLONDE WOMAN: Well, hurry up! I can't sit here all day!

The prisoner, exhausted, has a quiet voice, a natural dignity.

PRISONER: You must excuse me, Fräulein – These papers are very important to me. I don't like signing what I haven't read –

BLONDE WOMAN: Are you saying I've not taken down exactly what you dictated?

PRISONER: No – but I've go to make –

But he cannot finish – SMACK! – she leans across and hits him hard across the face, truly viciously.

BLONDE WOMAN: That is an insult!

The guard behind twitches, half moves.

GUARD: Fräulein. He won't be long.

Christabel stares at the blonde woman as she calmly covers her typewriter and tidies up her desk.

The prisoner signs the statement, on each page, and lifts his head to hand them back to the woman – the red mark from her vicious slap vivid on his cheek.

PRISONER: (*Quietly*) Thank you, Fräulein.

She ignores him. He tries to stand, but lurches badly, wincing in pain, and almost falls.

Christabel instinctively rises to help, but the guard motions her back with one word.

GUARD: Sit.

The prisoner shuffles slowly away, with the guard, passing by Christabel.

CHRISTABEL: (*Very soft*) God bless you.

His sunken eyes register it, and gleam momentarily.

The blonde woman is beginning to powder her nose, looking at herself in the mirror of her compact.

Her powdering slows, stops, her eyes swivel away from the compact. She has become aware of Christabel's genuinely hate-filled, unwavering stare –

The blonde holds Christabel's stare for a moment, then lowers her eyes, clicks shut her pretty compact, gathers up her handbag, and strides out. Past Christabel, who continues to glare.

A CLERK: Frau Bielenberg.

Christabel stands, her eyes hot with rage.

Arc lights behind a desk, focused on the door, but at first their dazzle conceals everything.

A VOICE: Heil Hitler, Frau Bielenberg. Sit down, please.

CHRISTABEL: Heil Hitler, Herr Kriminalrat Lange. I *would* sit,
     but I can't see a thing! These lights! Kindly turn them off.

This sounds patrician English upper class.

    Silence. Apart from the sound of Lange's rather deep breathing.
Dazzle. Then – CLICK! – to reveal, as the arc lamps die –

A youngish man, Lange, behind the desk, staring back at Christabel, unblinkingly. She speaks crisply.

CHRISTABEL: Thank you so much.

He says nothing, keeps staring, and, with a slight hesitation, quickly masked, she sits opposite him. He still stares. Silence. Then –

    It is good of you to give me some of your valuable time, Herr
      Kriminalrat.

He does not respond, and keeps staring at her, unnervingly. Again, she has to break an oppressive silence.

    I am really here to help you. I know you are only trying to
    discover the truth. That is why I have volunteered for this –
    interrogation.

LANGE: (*At last*) Help me? How?

CHRISTABEL: The one thing that has been bothering me since my
    husband's arrest is the fact that I am a foreigner. Of course, I
    have total – *absolute* – confidence in German justice, and I think
    if this had happened in England and I were German it would be –

Her voice fading, to let in remembered instructions

LEXI'S VOICE: *Say anything. Promise anything. It's your only chance.*

Tapping a pencil, like a metronome, Lange stares at her.

CHRISTABEL: – and even our wedding cake was decorated with the English flag and the swastika –

LEXI'S VOICE: *Say anything. Promise anything.*

CHRISTABEL: – I can assure you that when war broke out our sense of frustration was unbounded. I followed the Führer's speeches word for word and when again and again he held out the olive branch to England and again and again met nothing but rebuff – I can assure you that if it was up to me our two nations would be as united today as my husband and I are united.

She finishes what was obviously a very long oration. He stares at her. But now his face twitches, almost as though he is trying to smile at her.

LANGE: A very pretty speech.

Christabel tries yet more, yet more.

CHRISTABEL: Oh, I know I'm not a very good advocate – I'm not trying to tell you anything but the – We were not concerned with politics. I mean, when you have young children and are trying to bring them up straight and true for the Fatherland – *their* Fatherland – their *only* land – (*Breaks off.*) But, then. You know all about that, don't you Herr Lange?

She waits.

LANGE: What do you mean?

CHRISTABEL: I had the very good fortune to travel down here today with your wife, Herr Lange, and your two charming daughters – Edeltraut and – um – Hilde – May I congratulate you. They are such sweet children.

LANGE: You think so?

CHRISTABEL: Oh, yes. Oh, definitely.

But her mind says –

CHRISTABEL'S VOICE: *The nasty little creeps – Careful. Careful. Careful. Don't overdo it – !*

98

LANGE: Frau Doktor Bielenberg. You are a woman of *some* sense, at least. But you do not seem to know your own husband, or be acquainted with his activities –

CHRISTABEL: (*Quickly*) My husband and I had no secrets between us. To me, his case is a clear one. He has never been interested in politics in his life. I know that!

Lange opens a desk drawer, dumps a bulging file on to the desk.

LANGE: Your husband is a fool.

CHRISTABEL: An innocent one. Naïve. Yes.

LANGE: He is a great big stupid slob of an idiot who has betrayed himself at every turn. Look at this file! There's not one page which does not contain evidence of his idiocy and guilt. A pretty patriot, indeed! I have here a list of your friends. Every one of them traitors. Trott, zu Solz, Moltke, Langbehn, Wartenberg, Trotha, so on, and so on – Are you going to sit there and tell me that when you met in their homes, or they in yours, that you had *no* political discussions of any kind with them?

CHRISTABEL: You may think it extraordinary but, yes, that's exactly what I'm going to tell you. I am not, never have been and never will be interested in politics. Men and women who discuss politics are quite simply *bores*. I won't have it! And neither will Peter. I love Germany. Peter loves Germany. That's good enough for us!

LANGE: (*Angrily*) Should be. It *should* be.

His unexpected little spurt of emotion seems to help –

CHRISTABEL: I totally agree!

A tiny silence. They look at each other. She times her remark to come just as he is about to speak.

For example.

LANGE: Yes.

Instead of what he was about to say.

Christabel has a faint smile, as she speaks, but we do not hear, because – in her thoughts –

LEXI'S VOICE: – *some of the rats have enough sense to be frightened out of their filthy skins – Talk about your connections in England.*

99

Lange is very, very startled.

LANGE: *Who?*

CHRISTABEL: Oh, he was always talking politics when he visited my home – my parents – my uncle – and though he was always extremely fond of me –

LANGE: (*Trying to be calm*) Frau Bielenberg –

CHRISTABEL: I *still* found it a *bore*, quite frankly. Yes?

LANGE: (*Carefully*) Frau Bielenberg. Did you say Winston Churchill?

CHRISTABEL: (*Lightly*) Yes. He was a – Well, I say *was*, of course, because I've had no contact since, oh –

LANGE: Winston Churchill.

CHRISTABEL: Yes, but of course I do not share his politics, or rather his – No matter how fond he might be of – He was not then in office, of course – I'm sorry. Have I said something wrong? Oh, God, I'm always putting my foot in it – (*With emphasis*) Herr Lange. If there is any way I can repay your kindness when this war is – (*Mock concern*) Herr Lange?

A strained little silence. Then –

LANGE: (*Shakily*) Frau Doktor Bielenberg. The interview is concluded.

CHRISTABEL: Oh, but –

LANGE: I have volunteered for the army. The Fatherland's hour of need is upon us.

CHRISTABEL: Indeed. Yes. They are at the gates.

LANGE: Before I go, however – At the gates. Yes. Yes. We must all –

He coughs. Clears his throat.

CHRISTABEL: Herr Kriminalrat. I was foolish to come here. But I am not a good liar and I cannot change what I have said.

LANGE: Before I go, I promise I will deal with the case of your husband. I cannot tell you what the outcome will be, but I will see that the matter is settled before I go. Thank you. That is all!

Christabel smiles sweetly. And stays, sitting. He is disconcerted by this, expecting her to rise. He squares off his papers, clears his throat.

CHRISTABEL: I wondered.

It is a statement, not a question.

LANGE: You wondered?
CHRISTABEL: My husband. I wondered if you would be so kind as
     to let me see him.
LANGE: (*Incredulous*) *See* him?
CHRISTABEL: Since I am here.

He leans back in his chair, and stares at her. She smiles at him
again, mock naïve.

Deeper within the camp, a party of six or seven men shuffle across
a small square. Three prisoners, the rest guards.
     The prisoners are pale, thin, elderly men, their crumpled suits
hanging about them in folds. They clutch their trousers, and
shuffle, because they have no braces, belts or shoelaces.

Christabel stands, tense, looking out on to the square and the
passing prisoners from a small window of another room within
the camp.
     The party comes into the building, and along a corridor which
passes this room, making looming shadows and a shuffling sound
as they pass the set of inner, mottled windows to her side.
     She sits. She looks all around the small, near cell-like, cheerless
room. There is, apart from her chair, a small desk and chair by
the door, and, opposite, a table and a bench.
     Christabel goes to the door, stoops a little, ear against it,
listening intently. Satisfied, if tense, she quickly runs her fingers
around the rail or ledge which breaks the join between walls and
ceiling. She upturns her chair, examines it, rights it, goes to the
desk, peers under it, then takes a lipstick holder from her
handbag, and rolls it under the bench and the table.

The bench is against a wall. Her fingers probe. They come up
against a tiny projection. She peers closer. It is a small
microphone.
     But almost exactly as she registers it, she hears the door
opening –
     So fast does she move that she bumps her head on the
underside of the bench.
CHRISTABEL: (*Deliberately*) Ow!

A dapper young security policeman, in dark green uniform, with a briefcase, standing in the doorway, stares at Christabel, who is on her hands and knees, emerging from under the bench.

POLICEMAN: What–are–you–doing?

Scrambling upright, Christabel holds out the lipstick holder.

CHRISTABEL: I dropped my lipstick – and then, of course, I had to go and bump my head. Wood upon wood.

He sort of smiles.

POLICEMAN: Sit down. Please.

CHRISTABEL: Yes. Of course. That would probably be safer.

She smiles sweetly at him. He sits at the desk. He stares. She affects not to notice. A moment, then –

POLICEMAN: (*Clearing his throat*) I am Kriminalkommissar John.

Christabel looks at him, steadily.

   I hope you had a pleasant journey.

CHRISTABEL: Thank you.

Silence. He covertly examines her.

POLICEMAN: I hope you – You must understand that you cannot pass or give anything to a prisoner – to your husband – without my examining it –

CHRISTABEL: I did not expect to see him. I would have brought some sausages.

POLICEMAN: Sausages?

CHRISTABEL: He likes sausages.

They are now, both, puzzled.

POLICEMAN: But – you have not brought any – no – Do you have anything else?

CHRISTABEL: Some photographs of the children.

POLICEMAN: Children?

CHRISTABEL: Our children.

POLICEMAN: Show them to me. Please.

Christabel takes out a small pack of snapshots from her handbag, and hands them over.

   The security policeman, at his desk, examines the pictures –

   They are all of Nicky and John, sometimes alone, sometimes together, and occasionally with Christabel, posed against the lovely Black Forest and village scenes, turning in the policeman's hands.

   Christabel's expression – gazing across at the policeman – is that of a young mother who sees her children under any kind of attack.

> (*Suddenly*) They are nice-looking boys. Are they good? Do they behave themselves?

Christabel quickly adjusting her expression.

CHRISTABEL: Yes. They do.

He smiles, shakes his head as at some secret little joke, and, rising, hands her back the snapshots.

Outside, a guard escorts Peter, who towers above him, and does not shuffle. But he has a limp now.

> He is led into the building –

As the door opens into the room, Christabel instantly jerks to her feet.

> Peter stands in the doorway for half a second, staring at her.

Then, released into joy, he comes towards her, hands outstretched.

> The guard stands back against the wall, and the security policeman keeps his eyes on them.

POLICEMAN: Sit down. Sit down on the bench, if you please.

Peter and Christabel, standing, hands clasped, looking silently and deeply into each other, simply do not hear.

PETER: Christabel.

His voice is near to a croak. His face is puffy, pallid. There are now streaks of grey in his hair. Tears spring at her eyes.

> The armed guard moves to them, prods.

GUARD: Sit on the bench.

Christabel and Peter, hands still clasped very tightly, eyes still locked, at last register the instruction, and do so.

> The guard moves back to the wall. The security policeman lifts up and opens his briefcase, takes out papers, appears to study them, diligently.

> Christabel and Peter still seem scarcely able to speak.

CHRISTABEL: (*Moved*) Peter. There is so much to tell you – Peter. Oh. My love. I don't know where to start. I don't know how to find the words.

She releases one of her hands, and, with the tips of her fingers, gently touches his face. A kind of shudder goes through him. He briefly closes his eyes. When he opens them, the deadness in them, the distant or unreachable ache, seems to lift. He smiles.

PETER: Christabel. Never mind *words*. Never mind. Christabel.
(*Whisper*) Christabel.

With a quick, almost imperceptible, flick of his head the security
policeman instructs the guard to step outside the room.

CHRISTABEL: The boys are well. Getting big and strong and –
They miss you. We –

Her voice falters. He smiles, and puts a finger to her lips.

PETER: (*Whisper*) I am stronger than I thought. And it is you who
is my strength.

The security policeman clears his throat, ostentatiously, and
stands, gathering up his papers.

POLICEMAN: You have fifteen minutes.

The door closes behind them. They are, for the moment, alone.
Peter twists his head – with difficulty, like one disguising physical
pain – to look at the closing door.

As he turns back, it is clear that he is about to say something of
a different order.

PETER: (*Urgently*) Listen –

But she quickly puts her hand across his mouth, speaking at the
same time, her eyes flashing warning.

CHRISTABEL: Frau Muckle has been an angel. I don't know how I
would have managed without her. (*Then, lip movement only*)
Microphone.

PETER: Yes. I don't know how I shall ever be able to return her
kindness to my family. (*Lip movement only*) *Where?*

As she speaks, Christabel swiftly indicates the underside of the
bench on which they sit.

CHRISTABEL: She is looking after Nicky and John – they get on
with her –

PETER: Yes. Good!

Which is an acknowledgement of her warning.

CHRISTABEL: But she has had bad news recently. Her sister,
down the valley, you remember?

PETER: (*Frown*) I –

CHRISTABEL: The one who had three sons in the army and – you
know. One of them played hide–and–seek with Nicky.

PETER: Hide and –

CHRISTABEL: And cracked his head in the shed, looking for
Nicky.

Peter stares, then –

PETER: The rake jumped up and bit him.

They smile at each other. But then her expression changes, and she squeezes his hand.

CHRISTABEL: Well. He has been – Oh, it's sad news. He was killed on the Russian front.

PETER: Killed? Or just reported missing?

CHRISTABEL: No. Definitely killed. Killed in action.

Peter twists his head away momentarily, then looks back, eyes steady, putting down his anguish.

PETER: Oh, the poor mother. The poor – Oh. The times. What times.

CHRISTABEL: (*Weeping, but speaks for the microphone*) But I think in many ways she must be proud, Frau Muckle's sister. She loves her country, and her son has died for it.

PETER: (*Sadly*) Yes. (*Then*) I do not hear much news here, but the Western front seems to be holding, thank God.

CHRISTABEL: There is talk of a new secret weapon –

PETER: Then let us keep hoping!

They both look towards the microphone.

CHRISTABEL: The children are skiing every day. And John now talks with the most wonderful Baden accent. (*Suddenly*) Peter! I don't know what to say to you or how to say it!

Outside, somewhere, klaxons sound.

PETER: We are not apart. These walls cannot separate us.

CHRISTABEL: The children!

Suddenly she remembers the snapshots in her bag. She gives them to him.

PETER: Oh. Thank you. Thank you!

He takes and pores over them as a starving man might upon slices of bread.

Christabel watches him as the emotions contend on his face.

CHRISTABEL: I hope you will tell Kriminalrat Lange how grateful I am that he has allowed me to see you.

PETER: (*Absorbed*) Yes – yes –

He is studying the photographs, hungrily.

CHRISTABEL: And that you –

She stops as the door opens. The security policeman stands there, the armed guard following.

POLICEMAN: I am sorry. I cannot allow any more time. Stand up!

Christabel's returning train is clanking very slowly into a badly damaged and virtually unlit Berlin station, a dark train approaching, like something in a nightmare.

The carriage has no glass in the window. Soldiers stand, gathering together their kit. The long platform slides darkly into view.
    As the press thins out, the door swinging open, Christabel is revealed. She sits still, almost like one who does not intend to get off the train. She is locked into herself, all but expressionless, cold, tired, empty.

In a pedestrian tunnel. Small lights set in the concrete nevertheless make long shadows as people pass along, coming from an underground station.
    Christabel walks slowly, reflectively. People overtake, pass, their shadows growing and receding, their feet making hard sounds, slap–slap, on the concrete.
    Propaganda posters hang unnoticed in red and black tatters, shadowy on the pitted walls: 'Führer, we thank you!' and 'To victory with our Leader' and 'National Socialist order or Bolshevik chaos?
    Further along, as the dank passage uptilts towards the street, a workman is cleaning off some subversive graffiti – 'Medals for atrocity' and 'Soldiers! Desert!' and 'Down with Nazi brutality'.

Out of the tunnel, into the remnants of a street, with the rubble neatly piled to make a path. Some buildings still stand. Christabel finds herself in front of what is still recognizably the cinema where she and Peter had seen the film celebrating the defeat of France.
    She stops. She looks at the remains of the foyer, where the frames still (in parts) show scenes from a movie. And she remembers –
NEWSREEL VOICE: *Germans! Unfurl the flags! Let church bells ring!*

In the remembered cinema, huge against the half-silhouettes of the audience, the screen is full of Nazi flags and banners and, then, a beaming Hitler.

NEWSREEL VOICE: *Give highest honour to the Greatest Warlord of All Time!*

Row upon row, the audience erupts in wild applause and cheers and whistles and foot-stamping.

The tumultuous applause sounds, in a crescendo, over the badly damaged, near-gutted cinema.

And finally dies on Christabel's face, which shows no triumph, and little besides exhaustion and emptiness.

Air-raid sirens suddenly begin their terrible wail.

The sky is suddenly vivid as a phosphor bomb explodes, making everything garish, even Dante-esque, bathed in a green glow.

Heavy THUMP-WHUMPF! of near bombs. Sound of ack-ack batteries. Criss-crossing searchlights –

– and people running, for shelter, past ruined houses with boarded windows, heaps of rubble, blown-in walls, and the garish light shows some of the houses to be like open-fronted dolls' houses, revealing oddly pathetic glimpses of furnishings and decorations within.

Finding Christabel, following scurrying pedestrians. An arrow, saying PUBLIC AIR-RAID SHELTER points down a side-street.

As Christabel plunges down the side-street, she is disconcerted to find that – unexpectedly – she is alone. All the others seem to have disappeared, as though by magic. It feels creepy.

There is, just above her, a long drawn-out and extremely piercing whistle – almost what would now be considered an electronic one – and then a tremendous explosion, shaking everything.

Instantly, a gust of sudden wind rockets along, and Christabel is falling, falling –

Christabel has in fact been blown bodily down a flight of steps and heavily across the lap of a little old lady sitting in a narrow concrete-sided trench, dug out of a backyard, and covered with a tin roof. A very basic shelter, as near to a grave as to a haven.

OLD LADY: (*Moan*) Allmächtiger Gott, oh Heiland.

Christabel is stunned. But she gasps, clambers off the half-crushed old woman, choking down dust and apologies.

CHRISTABEL: I'm – oof! – I'm, oh God, I'm sorry. I'm so sorry. I
    don't know what –

The rest of her startled, confused speech is lost by another
high-pitched scream, a juddering explosion, and another
shocking blast of wind, which takes away most of the tin roof and
chips off fragments of concrete from the side of the trench.

    Then, suddenly, a sort of calm. The old lady calmly rights her
pork-pie hat.

OLD LADY: (*Loudly, firmly*) Eight. Peace now until the next wave
    comes over.

She removes her feet from the wall opposite.

CHRISTABEL: Eight? What has eight got to do with it?

OLD LADY: Eight bombs in each bomb cradle. And we were
    obviously in direct line.

She says this with the satisfaction of one who likes all things to be
precisely in order.

CHRISTABEL: I hope I didn't hurt you –

OLD LADY: Oh, quite like the old days, my dear. One never knew
    who was going to drop in unexpectedly.

Christabel looks at her. And then starts to laugh. Her companion
is clearly a game old bird.

CHRISTABEL: How long do you think this will go on for, the raid?

OLD LADY: Not long. An hour, perhaps two. An American carpet
    raid.

CHRISTABEL: 'Nose to tail. Nose to tail.'

OLD LADY: Almost. (*Sniff of disdain.*) They send over high-flying
    pathfinder planes, which drop those lights. Christmas trees.

CHRISTABEL: Nice present!

OLD LADY: They drop them at each corner of a large square –
    one, two, three, four – (*She draws a square in the dust with the
    toe of her shabby button-boot.*) And then, my dear, over come
    the heavy bombers and drop everything they've got into the
    square. (*Peers at Christabel.*) But where have *you* been? Don't
    you know these things? Were you no good at trigonometry in
    your studies?

CHRISTABEL: (*Smile*) I've been in the country. Deep in the Black
    Forest.

OLD LADY: Clever girl!

Their faces are suddenly illuminated by green light.

CHRISTABEL: O–oh.

OLD LADY: The British come by day and then the Americans come at night. And then the British come at night and the Americans by day. I wonder if they ever talk to each other?

A humming roar is clearly advancing upon them.

CHRISTABEL: Here they come.

OLD LADY: Oh, Schnucki, Schnucki. My Schnucki is all alone in the flat! (*She cocks her ear, changing back to her former tone.*) Yes. Here they come indeed.

WHUMPF!
   One!

WHUMPF!
   Two!

The enormous explosions, shaking the sides of the trench, are advancing upon them.

CHRISTABEL: Three!

WHUMPF! yet closer, and a banshee howl and whip of air. Rubble rattles down into the trench, covering them with dust. They cough and splutter.

   WHUMPF! again, even louder.

OLD LADY: Four!

WHUMPF! yet closer. More rubble. The remaining section of roof flies away. The sky above them is screaming. The light is ghastly.

CHRISTABEL: Five!

They look at each other, and suddenly they are in each other's arms, convinced that there will be no 'six' for them, except in the bits and pieces of their own shattered bodies.

OLD LADY: (*Cry*) Schnucki, Schnucki, my darling –

CHRISTABEL: (*Gabble*) Oh God look after Peter look after the children look after –

The next explosion must seem as though it obliterates everything, or turns it all upside down. The noise, the debris, the light, the screams of two trapped women.

   But then the dust cloud settles. Two dust-covered silhouettes begin to take human shape.

   The seventh explosion is, although shattering, clearly going beyond them.

   Christabel and the old lady cough, splutter and choke, and,

getting some of the filth out of their eyes and their mouths, get some sort of sight of each other.

OLD LADY: Eight.

Said calmly enough as the last of that particular stick shakes the ground again, but no sooner said than both women compulsively embrace each other, clinging together, and weeping for the joy of, after all, being alive.

They break, mutually a little embarrassed. The tears are rivulets in the caking mud on their faces.

That's the nearest I have ever had – (*Cough, sob*) – the very nearest –

CHRISTABEL: (*Half-laugh*) We *are* alive – aren't we?

The old lady adjusts her pork-pie hat again, sending out a cloud of dust, then taps it on the top of her head, crisp and decisive.

OLD LADY: An extremely expensive method of trying to kill us, don't you think? They must be made of money! I will never go out late without my Schnucki again. Poor Schnucki!

CHRISTABEL: Schnucki is your – um – husband – ?

OLD LADY: Schnucki is not a person. Schnucki is my dog. My dachshund.

CHRISTABEL: Oh.

OLD LADY: And mostly superior to any person, in my experience. My *long* experience. Present company excepted, of course, my dear.

Christabel smiles, and nods. The entrance to the shelter, beyond the steps, glows yellow and orange as the fires take hold. Smoke drifts across them.

The skyline is still ablaze, and a vehicle in the road has been turned into a heap of twisted metal. The damage all around, smoking and smouldering, is terrible.

Small domestic items skeeter and flap and clang in the disturbed air.

Christabel emerges out of a pall of smoke, turning this way, that way, trying to get bearings, as the sky reddens into a grisly dawn.

Walking now along the road where she used to live, Christabel is clearly worn out, and still grubbily dust-covered from her time in the shelter.

She examines the damage to the houses, the crater in the road, the changes, and remembers –

NEISSE'S VOICE: *We be one land now. Germany and Austria. One people. One leader. Ay – we got us the right man in charge now, ant us?*

Christabel pushes open the broken gate and enters the garden of her former home.

NEISSE'S VOICE: *All is lovely in the garden, Frau Bielenberg!*

CHRISTABEL: (*Quietly, as though addressing Neisse*) Are you talking about the blossom or the thorns?

The old garden is now a total mess. The lawn has been dug up to grow vegetables. There is a small crater where the bushes had been, from incendiary bombing.

NEISSE'S VOICE: *Ah – but we shall burn the thorns! Cut 'em down! Set light to 'em! We got us a good gardener now, Frau Bielenberg!*

Moved, exhausted, out of touch with herself, and buffeted by memory, Christabel goes to the rusted and buckled remains of the children's swing.

She pushes the half of seat that is left, so that it creak–creaks more or less as it used to. Tears rim her eyes. She is unaware that she is being closely observed –

From the old living room, unknown faces of young people are virtually pressed against the criss-crossed tape on the glass of the french windows looking out on to the garden, watching strange Christabel.

Creak–creak goes the damaged swing, from a momentarily damaged Christabel.

But, surfacing into reality, she becomes aware that there are people inside the house in which she had for so long lived.

She stops the swing, and crosses the damaged garden, in order to peer in at the french windows.

The light makes it difficult for her to see in properly. She can see vague shapes and movements. She tenses. And then she tap–taps against the taped glass –

Several young men are staring out at her. One of them is attending to the pan that is bubbling on an oil stove against the now stained and discoloured wall.

The room is full of contraband goods, like a smuggler's den.

FIRST YOUTH: (*In Dutch*) Who the hell is it?

SECOND YOUTH: (*In Dutch*) Perhaps she's off her head. Look how dirty she is!

THIRD YOUTH: (*In Dutch*) Yes – pretty, though. Let her in!

The first youth pushes open the door, with a severe expression. He speaks 'German' (i.e. English) in a marked accent.

FIRST YOUTH: Who are you? What do you want here, pretty lady?

CHRISTABEL: I – this was my house, and –

SECOND YOUTH: (*Sharp*) Name? What is the name?

CHRISTABEL: Bielenberg. Christabel Bielenberg.

Everyone seems to relax. She is engulfed, pulled in, sat down, and bomb dust brushed off her shoulders.

FIRST YOUTH: You are the wife of Peter? His lady?

CHRISTABEL: Yes. I –

FIRST YOUTH: How is Peter? Where is he?

CHRISTABEL: Ravensbrück.

An instant silence. Then they flock around her again.

SECOND YOUTH: A drink. You want a drink.

THIRD YOUTH: Something to eat?

FOURTH YOUTH: Anything you want! A bath? A hot bath maybe, maybe?

She stares at them, amazed, like one in a dream.

CHRISTABEL: But – but who are you all – ? Where do you come from – ?

FIRST YOUTH: We are Dutch.

THIRD YOUTH: From Rotterdam.

SECOND YOUTH: We are from the Forced Labour Force –

CHRISTABEL: The – what?

FIRST YOUTH: They make us come to work. Without our permission.

SECOND YOUTH: So we steal. We break out. We live as *we* want – With *our* permission.

FIRST YOUTH: Your husband say we live here. Keep your heads down, he say.

THIRD YOUTH: Good man! Good man!

FIRST YOUTH: Why is he in Ravensbrück? How did they catched him?

Again, an instant silence. They watch her, carefully.

CHRISTABEL: I have just been there. And I – I –

The long-delayed reaction sets in. She looks as though she is about to collapse.

I'm sorry. I was caught in a raid. I have not slept.

FIRST YOUTH: Don't talk. Not now. You have bath. You have sleep.

FOURTH YOUTH: The coffee is coming now.

SECOND YOUTH: Go to sleep, why not? All in good time!

FIRST YOUTH: You want hot-water bottle? You want music? You want silk stockings, maybe, why not?

Christabel, recovering herself, looks at them in wonder. Then –

CHRISTABEL: I have a long journey to make. Back to my children. I came to see if the house was still standing, and, if it was, to see my – Peter's and my bedroom, and –

A sudden spurt of emotion, like a pain, and she cannot finish. They all look at her, not knowing what to do. Then –

FOURTH YOUTH: Here. Please. You drink.

He has made the coffee. She takes the huge mug, gratefully –

CHRISTABEL: Oh, thank you, thank you –

Holding both hands around the mug, she sips. Her expression changes –

(*Astonished*) But – but this is *real* coffee!

FIRST YOUTH: (*Severely*) But of course.

A beat. Then they all roar with laughter. And then Christabel joins in.

SECOND YOUTH: (*Awkwardly*) You are a nice lady with a nice husband.

FIRST YOUTH: (*Awkwardly*) We, too, will pray that he will come back safe and sound.

Christabel's and Peter's former bedroom is perhaps the least affected by change in this now strange house.

Christabel, alone now, and dressed as though ready to go, sits on the bed, remembering everything in the thin, rapidly fading, wintry light.

A moment. Then –

CHRISTABEL: Peter.

Silence. She seems to wait. Then goes across to the window, which is partly stuffed with cardboard and sacking.

Below, in the darkening and wintry garden, the children's swing creak–creaks, as of old.

In pained reverie, Christabel tries to peer down into the damaged garden.

(*Quietly to herself*) No. Not us. Not between us. Never.

From far off, over the city, the air-raid sirens begin. Almost at once, the sky is pierced with searchlights and the far ring of anti-aircraft guns begin to pound.

Footsteps sound on the now bare-boarded stair, running.

A knock–knock on the door. Christabel does not answer. Knock–knock again.

Then, at her non-response, the door tentatively opens. The first youth comes half in, stops, looks at Christabel, who is absolutely still at the window.

FIRST YOUTH: Frau Bielenberg?

Christabel does not turn.

Christabel!

She looks at him, as though coming from a long way away, and smiles.

CHRISTABEL: You know, there used to be a nightingale in this garden.

FIRST YOUTH: You must come! Shelter!

She smiles again, and shakes her head.

CHRISTABEL: No.

FIRST YOUTH: But there is a raid! You must not stay in here.

CHRISTABEL: But I must.

FIRST YOUTH: No. No. Is silly!

CHRISTABEL: I shall be gone as soon as it is light. But I want to stay in this room. Until then, I want to stay here. (*A brilliant smile*.) Don't worry about me.

He looks at her, and seems about to remonstrate, but then suddenly comprehends.

FIRST YOUTH: Yes. Yes. I understand.

He quietly closes the door.

The raid has well and truly started. The lights in the sky reflect on the bedroom walls, garishly, menacing. She sits on the bed again, perfectly composed, perfectly still.

Spring has come to a breathtakingly beautiful vista of hills, woodland, and old Black Forest houses.

Outside the inn, as sunshine glows and dapples through the window, the bell rings on the steeple.

On the road up to the village, clip–clop, as the milk cart and Bausch bring the empty churns back.

Legs dangling over the side, Peter sits on the back of the cart, between the churns. He looks ill. But he is also grinning, helplessly, like an idiot.

The retreating Wehrmacht is now in evidence. A long trench runs down the street. Armoured staff cars are in line at the inn. Trucks are just discernible beyond.

The arriving milk cart – '*Whoa!*' – stops at the inn. And it can be seen there is no Peter aboard.

Bausch calls, loudly.

BAUSCH: Frau Doktor Bielenberg! Frau Bielenberg!

Soldiers digging at the trench watch him with a mild interest.

In the main room of the inn: three stiff figures, faces almost hidden by the huge fur collars of their greatcoats, pore over maps laid across temporary tressle. Flashes of red braid, gleam of polished boots: very high officers, murmuring.

BAUSCH: – Frau Bielenberg!

Christabel has to pass through.

CHRISTABEL: Excuse me. Please.

They stop talking, look at her, return to their maps, ignoring Frau Muckle and her tray of coffee mugs.

Outside, a heavy artillery piece, drawn by horses, is arriving, and another car full of officers, a truck of troops, and a huge bustle of military activity, as Christabel comes out to Bausch.

Bausch, looking about, leans down from the cart, and starts to whisper in her ear.

But even as Christabel's face starts to transform, there is a loud hooting from one of the military vehicles.

A SERGEANT: (*Bellow*) Come on! Come on! Get that cart out of here! Move it! Or you'll get a bullet up your arse!

With a shrug, Bausch gees up the horse, and the cart trundles.

Christabel, astonished, looks at it move, then –

CHRISTABEL: (*Cry*) *What*? *What* did you –

She manages to stop herself, runs after the milk cart.

The German army truck comes up alongside. She climbs up on the cart. The soldiers whistle at her, but oddly without conviction.

Away from the village and its military activity, Peter comes out of the deep trees into the clearing. He has great difficulty in walking.

Bausch's log cabin is in the clearing. Peter reaches it. He leans against it for a moment, wincing with pain, looks about.

And laughs. Enough to make a bird trill in alarm. The sudden trill makes him cautious. He cocks his head, listens, then goes on into the log cabin.

At the inn, Christabel whirls Frau Muckle around and around by the waist, utterly exuberant.

FRAU MUCKLE: (*Gasp*) Frau Bielenberg – ! Stop! Stop! I shall be giddy – !

CHRISTABEL: (*Too loud*) They let him out! They let him go! They let him go!

FRAU MUCKLE: Shh! Shh! The Devil will hear! Hans has told me. He is not safe yet. Be still! Stop it!

Christabel controls herself, but her face is streamed with tears of relief.

CHRISTABEL: They dumped him outside the gate with a travel warrant to a punishment squad in the army. Can you imagine? No escort!

FRAU MUCKLE: Frau Doktor! Do not make so much noise.

Christabel holds down her joy, hand to mouth.

CHRISTABEL: I can't seem to – I can't – oh dear God – !

FRAU MUCKLE: He'll need some food and coffee – We don't know how many days he will have to keep his head down.

CHRISTABEL: They might not come for him. They might forget all about him in the mess they're in now –

FRAU MUCKLE: The mess we're all in y'mean. Perhaps we'd be safer up in them woods as well.

CHRISTABEL: I must wait. I must wait till dark. Oh, bless the trees. God bless the trees!

Her excitement makes her clench and hug at Frau Muckle again.

FRAU MUCKLE: (*Dry*) Don't tell the trees. And don't tell the boys
    neither.

CHRISTABEL: Oh. But – No?

FRAU MUCKLE: They might let it out by mistake. They're too
    young. And – look – come see – All boys love the soldiers.

She is at the little window.

From window, Nicky and John, fascinated, are hand in hand
watching the noisy arrival of an army messenger on a spluttering
motorcycle.

The road is full of troops, squatting down, sprawling, playing
cards. Many of them very young.

One of the soldiers asks John to pick a card from the pack.

Christabel turns from the window.

CHRISTABEL: (*Tense*) But we have to be together, now. We have
    to go through the last bit together.

FRAU MUCKLE: Then don't go in the dark. Don't go through
    those woods at night. They'll shoot at anything that moves.

Christabel nods, quickly, and then starts to laugh again,
overwhelmed with joy.

Night and the woods. Military activity, deep in the trees. Silent
troops. Dark trees. Soft challenges.

An owl hoots. A sudden, sharp command from an NCO. A
flare suddenly hangs in the sky above the trees.

The log cabin is a dark little hump in the trees. Sounds of distant
gunfire, and then the whumph–whumph of artillery fire, very
close.

Inside, Peter drags himself to the open slit in the log wall to press
his eyes against it.

But there is nothing to be seen. Whumph–whumph again,
near.

On a rise opposite the inn, the artillery piece earlier manoeuvred
is firing down into the valley.

Within the inn, the noise is deafening. The two boys are clinging tight to her, as they half sit, half lie, blanket-wrapped, on her bed.

CHRISTABEL: It's all right. Everything will be all right.

She is still glowing within.

Day again, and a lull in artillery fire. Tinkle–tinkle of cowbells as the herd is still driven through the soldiers and their equipment towards pasture.

Apathetic Wehrmacht faces, weary, look at the passing cows.

In the inn, Christabel looks at the now sleeping children. She adjusts their covers.

CHRISTABEL: (*Whisper*) Not long. Not long.

From below, in the main room, a boy suddenly cries a desperate cry.

A boy soldier and Alois, the old man, are being taken out of the room full of officers and soldiers.

The boy is crying '*Mother! Mother – Mum! Mum –* !' in a horrible anguish and fear.

Frau Muckle comes to the kitchen door, her face appalled.

The high officers rise from their tables, not quite looking at each other, and move to the outside door, in a clatter of boots.

Frau Muckle goes close to one of the soldiers.

FRAU MUCKLE: What is it? What's going on – ?

SOLDIER: (*Morose*) They're to be shot!

FRAU MUCKLE: *What* – ?

SOLDIER: The boy tried to desert. Poor little bugger.

FRAU MUCKLE: Jesus and Holy God. He's just out of school!

SOLDIER: The old 'un refused to put up some telephone wire –
    Christ. Don't ask *me*.

FRAU MUCKLE: But *he's* not a soldier –

The soldier looks at her, moving away.

SOLDIER: We all are now. All of us.

FRAU MUCKLE: (*Hiss*) Bastards.

The soldier hears, looks back, says nothing.

Higher up, Christabel has gone to the window, drawn by peculiar noises.

The significance of what she is watching gradually becomes clear to her in a horrified incredulity.

She sees, on the rise opposite the inn, four soldiers with rifles waiting, while a still sobbing boy and apparently bewildered Alois are made to stand against a tree.

Rifles raise, rifles fire, the sobbing stops, the two bodies lie in small oozes of their own blood.

Then, out of the sky, a growing scream –

An American fighter plane is diving out of the morning sun, machine-gunning as it screams down and up.

Christabel hurls herself on top of the still sleeping boys.

Rat–a–tatt–tat–tatt! and the bullet holes trace a neat, fast line across the wall as the scream of the plane recedes.

NICKY: (*Muffled*) Mum – Mum. I – Mum. I can't *breathe* –

Later, a fat American tank is coming slowly up the magnificent incline towards the village.

On either side of the mountain road, moving in slow cautious line, the infantry accompanies the tank.

In the cabin in the woods, Peter leans hard against the wall, breathing heavily.

PETER: Christabel – Chris –

He coughs, putting his hand to his mouth, hard. As he takes his hand away, it is splattered with blood.

Beyond the log cabin, there is seemingly just a dense tangle of trees, but then a glimpse of flitting figures.

Christabel, with covered basket, Nicky and John, are moving like Scouts through the wood.

Sounds of battle, growing.

RADIO VOICE: *Germans! In proud reverence and sorrow we lower our flags before him.*

Another fighter plane launches itself out of the sky above the village in a screaming snarl, rat–a–tat–tat–tat.

The Wehrmacht trunks, pulling back, are hit.

WUMPH! from the German artillery piece. An answering shell blows a crater in the middle of the street.

RADIO VOICE: *With his passing, one of the greatest heroes of German history has left us. Germans! Adolf Hitler has perished. His struggle goes on!*

Bruckner's Seventh Symphony coming from radio, out across a street, littered now with German dead.

The solemn music coming from the inn's radio, but the room is now empty.

The announcement is repeated.

RADIO VOICE: *Germans! In proud reverence and sorrow we lower our flags before him –*

In a clearing in the forest, Christabel, Nicky and John are rushing out of the tree line towards Peter. They hug and kiss and laugh and weep, together again.

'I'm Following You' begins to play, sweetly insistent, its original resonances *almost* restored.